# Nighttime
# Parenting

# Nighttime Parenting

## How to Get Your Baby and Child to Sleep

William Sears, M.D.

*La Leche League International*
*Schaumburg, Illinois*

Revised edition, August 1999
©1985, 1999 by William Sears. All rights reserved.
Printed in the USA

Photo credits: frontispiece, Mark Ford; p. 9, Betsy Liotus; p. 29, 74,
122, 129, David Arendt; p. 51, Arm's Reach Co-Sleeper; p. 68,
© Jean Hoelscher; p. 87, Anne St. Laurent; p. 171, Barbara Beebe
Allen; p. 193, Pat Crosby; others, William Sears.

Illustrations: p. 161, Maurice Wagner; others, Carol Cuatt.

Cover design by Penguin USA
Book Layout: Digital Concepts, LLC
ISBN 0-912500-53-0
Library of Congress 99-63632

La Leche League International
1400 N. Meacham Road
P.O. Box 4079
Schaumburg, IL 60168-4079 USA
www.lalecheleague.org

Dedicated to my family:
Martha, James, Robert, Peter, Hayden, Erin,
Matthew, Stephen, Lauren.

# Contents

# Foreword

Dr. Sears, where were you when we needed you? If only you were older (much older), you could have written this wonderful book in the early days of La Leche League when we were new parents helping each other to unlearn the silly, illogical "rules" imposed on our own poor mothers by the pediatric gurus of their day.

It was clear that these doctors hadn't had much hands-on experience in parenting small babies. I still remember my mother-in-law describing the nights she spent sitting beside her baby's crib, tears running down her face because she did not dare pick up her poor screaming infant for fear of damaging his personality. (Fortunately she was smart and loving enough to defy the expert's mandates, and the baby turned out quite well after all. In fact, I married him.)

My own mother tells her children that all eight of us, with only one exception, slept through the night by age six weeks. The exception, my little brother, who wouldn't conform to the rules, required a full three months of shutting out piteous wails before he slept through. Despite this, a mother's natural concern about her children's welfare came to our rescue, and we didn't turn out too badly either.

Today, thank heaven, mothers have Dr. Bill Sears who knows whereof he speaks. "Believe me," he seems to say, "I've been there." And we do believe him, as his love for children and knowledge of their needs is evident throughout his book. It goes hand in glove with La Leche League's philosophy echoing the convictions expressed in THE WOMANLY ART OF BREASTFEEDING. Most important is his respect for the institution of marriage and family. Babies need mothers and fathers, he says. They do best within a solid family structure.

Dr. Sears' section on working mothers is sure to be helpful to the mother who must be away from her child part of the time. Yet he knows that full-time mothering is better for babies, and he doesn't hesitate to say so.

How reassuring Dr. Sears is, too, about the things mothers worry about—the fears parents have about Sudden Infant Death Syndrome, for example. What he says here is true. There are fewer SIDS deaths among babies who are breastfed and perhaps also among babies who sleep with their mothers. Mothers have a special sixth sense when it comes to their little nursing babies. I believe that, asleep or awake, a nursing mother is always tuned in to her baby in a special way. I pray that those new mothers who say they just can't sleep with the baby next to them will heed what Dr. Sears says and will give sleeping with baby a fair trial. It does work, and ultimately everyone is happier.

Reading NIGHTTIME PARENTING brought back many memories. We were the parents back then who knew that the old way—letting baby cry it out—was wrong, but we were totally inept at resolving the problem. There I was, pacing the floor at three in the morning with this screaming infant, feeling as if I would never get enough sleep again in my whole life and struggling to overcome a wild urge to throw the baby out the nearest window. Now the thing that strikes me is that despite the many nighttime hours I spent fearing I would never sleep again, today, many years later, I have almost forgotten them. I actually did catch up on my sleep, though it took me a while to learn not to try to fit small children into an adult mold. Our little ones did sleep with us eventually, and we retired the crib. There was a transitional mattress on the floor when an energetic toddler who needed sprawl space spent a good part of the night with elbows and knees in her parents' ribs or faces. (Back then we hadn't even heard of queen-size mattresses!)

I would gladly have traded in all the screaming nightmares the older children experienced for a few kicks in the face. When the younger ones were four- and five-year-olds, bedtime no longer included checking under the bed for monsters. They knew there was nothing there but dust balls.

Today's young parents, those in the middle of the coping years, need to know that their efforts will pay off. Knowing the whys and wherefores of babies' behavior helps tremendously to keep us going and helps us to accept and even enjoy these hours and hours and hours of full-time parenting. The rewards do come, maybe not right away, but later. I recall the words of Dr. Herbert Ratner, La Leche League's mentor over the years, who observed, "It is better to lose sleep over your children when they are little than to have to stay up worrying about them when they are older."

This book belongs on the shelf right next to THE WOMANLY ART OF BREASTFEEDING. It will help all new parents raise happier and more secure children who, having learned from birth that the people they love most of all, their parents, can be depended on, are confident and secure about moving out into the world on their own. Needs that have been met and satisfied are not still begging for resolution. These children are free to grow up, to move on, and to be their own persons. Best of all, they are equipped with invaluable first-hand experience in family living which they can share and pass on to their children when the time comes.

Thank you, Dr. Sears, from a grandma who learned it the hard way.

Mary White
Founder, La Leche League International

# Introduction

"If only I could get one full night's sleep!" This is the plea of millions of tired parents who struggle nightly with the dilemma of wanting to be a good nighttime parent yet long for a full night's sleep.

Many nighttime parents are confused about the conflict between what they feel and what they hear from friends, relatives, and doctors. When their child awakens at 3:00 A.M. (for the third time that night), their parental intuition says to get up and console the crying child. Advice from outsiders says "Let the baby cry it out." Who is right? I have written NIGHTTIME PARENTING to help parents answer this question.

When I started pediatric practice, I was faced with the reality that doctors receive the least training in the problem areas which bother parents the most. "Doctor, is it all right for our baby to sleep in our bed?" "When our baby wakes up crying, should I go to him or am I going to spoil him?" These were real concerns from real people and they deserved real answers. But I didn't know the answers. There aren't any courses in medical school on where babies should sleep or why babies cry.

At the time my wife and I were new parents ourselves, struggling to develop our own parenting style. We read the baby books but came away feeling confused. The respected prophets of childcare took the easy way out. They offered quick and easy advice. "If your baby cries one hour the first night, forty-five minutes the second, thirty minutes the third night, by the fourth night he'll go right to sleep." This rigid advice did not sit right with me, but I wasn't sure why. I couldn't bring myself to practice it on my own children, and therefore, I certainly wasn't going to offer this advice to my patients. And so I learned very early in my practice that most problems in child-rearing do not have easy answers.

Then one day, a wise colleague took me aside and confided that when he wanted to know the answer to a difficult question on parenting, he asked an experienced, intuitive mother. Eureka! A simple idea, but a good one. I resolved that I would learn from experienced mothers. In particular, I set out to learn the answers to the following questions about sleep:

*Why do some families have fewer sleep problems than others?*

*Why do some children sleep better?*

*Why do some parents cope better than others?*

*What works for most parents most of the time and why?*

Whenever I interviewed a parent who had answers to these questions, I kept notes on what worked and what didn't work. When I became even more interested in the particular question of coping with nighttime parenting, I sent out a questionnaire to parents whose advice I trusted. In NIGHTTIME PARENTING I will share with you the advice that over 5,000 parents have shared with me.

Through the years I have also been blessed with eight children and a wife who is an intuitive mother. My own theories of how babies should sleep have been put into practice. The parenting styles that I advocate in this book are those which I have personally worked with—and slept with. They work!

Sleep problems occur when your child's night-waking exceeds your ability to cope. NIGHTTIME PARENTING is directed at both of these variables: lessening your child's night-waking and increasing your ability to cope. Much of this book is devoted to helping you understand that babies and children do what they do because they were "designed" that way. For example, I will help you understand why babies are not designed to sleep through the night.

One of the goals of this book is to help parents and children achieve sleep harmony. I have enough faith in parents' intuition and in babies' abilities to signal their needs to believe that if the caller and the receiver can get their communication network working, sleep harmony will result. This is not a "let your baby cry it out" book. This is a "learn how to listen and respond" book. When you have achieved this sensitivity and harmony, you will enjoy your child, and your child will feel secure and loved.

Difficult sleepers can exhaust the whole family, put a strain on their parents' marriage, and contribute to parent burnout. Parent burnout is seldom the fault of the child. It is the fault of a society in which there has been a breakdown of the extended family, the parents' traditional support system. Not since frontier days has a mother been expected to do so much for so many with so little emotional support. In NIGHTTIME PARENTING I will offer suggestions on how to avoid parent burnout and how to develop a support system that gives mothers an extra set of arms in caring for their babies and gives fathers the opportunity to make a real difference.

Throughout this book I have noted studies in sleep theory which have practical implications for understanding and surviving your baby's nighttime needs. I have included real-life situations with creative ideas for coping with sleepless nights and crying babies, as well as stories from nighttime parenting in my own family. Pediatricians are not uniquely blessed with easy sleepers. I, too, have spent many hours in nighttime fathering.

## *How to Read this Book*

In order to get the greatest benefit (and the most sleep) out of this book, I advise expectant parents and parents of newborns to read the entire book with a view toward preventing serious sleep problems. For parents whose children already sleep poorly, this book can be used as a reference for handling specific nighttime problems. I hope this book will also be helpful for persons who are in the position of offering advice on nighttime parenting, such as grandparents, counselors, and health care professionals. Remember, new parents are particularly vulnerable to childcare advice because they love their child and respect their advisor. I am confident that NIGHTTIME PARENTING will help advisors keep this respect.

It has been fourteen years since the publication of the first edition of this book. In that time, we have added three more children and four grandchildren to our family. We continue to see that meeting babies' nighttime needs pays off. Our kids and our grandkids all sleep well and have good sleep habits. The time our babies spent in our arms, at mom's breasts, and in our bed has been just a small part of their lives, yet the memories of our love and constant availability will last a lifetime. The benefits even extend to the next generation.

William Sears, M.D.
April, 1999

# Chapter 1

# Attachment Parenting: A Style that Works

Each day, expectant couples come into my office with eager questions. "This is our first baby. We really want to do right by our child. Can you give us some tips on getting a good start?" I answer these couples by offering a style of parenting that works for most couples most of the time—attachment parenting. Nighttime parenting is one part of this total parenting style.

Attachment parenting helps a mother and father achieve two main goals:

1. *To know their child.*
2. *To help their child feel right.*

A child who feels right acts right and is a joy to parent. I want you as parents to enjoy your child.

## What Is Attachment Parenting?

One way to tell you more about attachment parenting is to share with you some attachment tips. This is the advice I give new parents in my practice who are eager to get a good start. These tips can help you know and understand your child so that you can help him feel right.

### Make a Commitment

Very early in your parenting career, before the birth of your baby, make a commitment. Promise your faithful attention to two relationships: to yourselves as a married couple and to your child as his parents. One of the greatest gifts you can give your new baby is a home built on the foundation of a stable and fulfilled marriage.

To strengthen these commitments during pregnancy, I advise couples to follow a custom we have enjoyed in our own family. I suggest that each night before going to bed you as a couple lay your hands on the pregnant uterus. Talk about your commitment to each other as a married couple and your commitment to this tiny life inside. This beautiful nighttime ritual gets to be a habit that is likely to continue after your baby arrives. After the birth of our baby, I had become so accustomed to laying my hands on my unborn baby that I couldn't get to sleep at night unless I would go over and lay my hand on the head of our little newborn and reaffirm my commitment to fathering her. I was hooked! I was already attached before our infant was born.

### Create a Peaceful Womb Experience

In the past twenty years there have been new and exciting discoveries about the fetus's sensory and emotional awareness. Mother and her unborn baby share emotions. When mother is upset, baby may be upset. If your pregnancy is cluttered with emotional stress (especially the last three months), you have a higher risk of having a child who is anxious, and an anxious child has a high risk of being a difficult sleeper. By creating a peaceful pregnancy experience you begin creating harmony with your baby. Thus prenatal harmony may well carry over into the baby's sleep patterns.

### Prepare Yourselves

Many couples spend a lot of time and money preparing the properly appointed nursery. Your baby could care less what his or her room looks like. He wants you, so prepare yourselves. Parent support groups can assist you in this preparation by helping you arrive at a parenting style that best fits your level of commitment and your own family situation. In my opinion, the most effective parent support organization is **La Leche League International,** a worldwide mother-to-mother communication network. La Leche League is especially effective in explaining the concept of attachment parenting because of the information and support it provides for breastfeeding mothers. I advise new mothers to join this organization early in their parenting careers, preferably during pregnancy.

An important part of preparing yourself is to take a good **prepared childbirth** class and select your birthing options wisely. Choose a birthing environment which encourages you to stay in tune with your body during labor. Mothers who are properly prepared to decode their body's signals (for example, when to move around and when to lie still) and who give birth

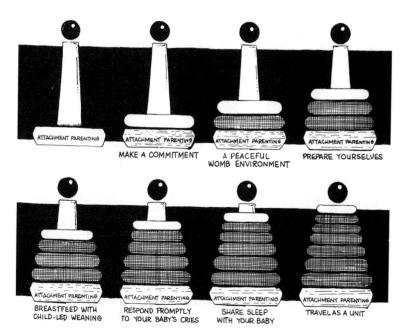

in an environment which allows them the freedom to do so are more likely to become quickly attached to their babies. Mothers who have a birthing experience where fear and lack of control predominate may have more difficulty forming an immediate attachment. There is also a higher risk of having a difficult sleeper if you have a difficult labor and delivery.

## Breastfeed with Natural Weaning

Breastfeeding encourages attachment and helps you take cues from your baby. It encourages you to watch your baby for signs of needing food and comfort rather than watching the clock and counting ounces. You and your baby will learn to know each other better and will be more in harmony with one another.

I have a sign in my office that says, "Early weaning not recommended for infants." New mothers are vulnerable to careless comments of well-meaning friends and relatives who exclaim, "What, you're still nursing?" Part of understanding the general philosophy of attachment parenting is understanding the real meaning of the term weaning. Parents often think of weaning as a loss of a relationship, a detachment. Weaning is really not a negative term but a very positive one. In ancient writings, the term meant "to ripen." It is a feeling of fulfillment and readiness whereby a child looks up to his mother and says or feels, "I am ready. I am filled with this relationship and ready to pass on to another one. Thanks, Mom."

Life is a series of weanings—weaning from the womb, weaning from the breast, weaning from parents' bed or crib, weaning from home to school, from school to work. Whenever a child is weaned from any of these places of security before he is ready, he is at risk of developing what I call behaviors of premature weaning. These stem from an underlying feeling of "not right" and include anger, aggression, and moodiness, all of which can stay with the child through life.

Don't limit your breastfeeding to a predetermined number of months, what I call **calendar parenting**. As long as both parties of the nursing couple enjoy this relationship, then nurse until both of you are filled. Calendar parenting simply does not work, and it often produces a short-term gain for a long-term loss. It is much more realistic for parents to enter their parenting careers without any preconceived expectations of when a child should give up a certain need. The rate at which babies develop physically and emotionally varies tremendously. Having rigid and unrealistic expectations will only lead to frustration, which can put a damper on your spontaneous interaction with your child and ultimately lessen your enjoyment. More importantly, imposing restraints on your child's source of security can have long-lasting effects on his physical and mental well-being.

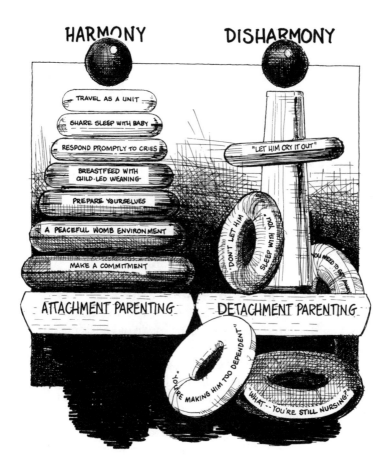

## Respond Promptly to Your Baby's Cries

Every baby comes wired with an ability to signal his needs.
Adults call this unique language the cry. Every mother develops
the "wiring" necessary to receive her baby's signal. This is a
special communication network designed for the survival of the
baby and the development of the mother. Promptly responding
to your baby's cries increases your sensitivity to your baby.
Sensitivity helps develop your parental intuition.

## Be Open to Trying Various Sleeping Arrangements

Babies often give their parents cues as to where they want to
sleep. Some babies sleep best in their own rooms; others sleep
best in a bed in their parents' room; many babies sleep best in
their parents' bed. Parents have varying preferences as well.
The sleeping arrangement whereby all three of you (mother,
father, and baby) sleep best is the right one for your individual
family. Your baby trusts that you are open and receptive to the
cues that he is giving you about where he needs to sleep. You
are also trusting yourself to respond to your baby's needs for a
certain sleeping arrangement even though this may not be in
accordance with the norms of your neighborhood. One of the
most important pieces of baby furniture I advise new parents to
purchase is a king-size bed. Welcoming your baby into your bed
is just another part of a parenting style of trust and openness. If
sleeping with your baby feels right to you and is working, then
it is okay. As with any feature of a parenting style, if it is not
working and does not feel right, then drop it.

## Travel as a Father-Mother-Baby Unit

While traveling on a speaking tour of Australia I began to
appreciate the "marsupial mothering" style of kangaroos, whose
babies are nearly always in touch with the mother because they
live in a pouch on the mother's abdomen. I advise couples not
to succumb to the usual outside pressure to "get away from
your baby," but instead to become accustomed to "wearing" the
baby in an infant sling or baby carrier. As you get used to being
a unit you will feel right when you are together and not right
when you're apart. Functioning together by day makes it easier
to function together by night.

### Beware of Detachment Parenting

This is a restrained style of parenting that warns parents against taking cues from their child. The advocates of detachment parenting preach: "Let the baby cry it out. He has to learn to sleep through the night." "Don't be so quick to pick your baby up. You're spoiling her." "Get your baby on a schedule. He's manipulating you." "Don't let your baby in your bed. You're creating a terrible habit." Besides being full of negatives, this style of parenting also features quick and easy recipes for difficult problems. For example, when a baby repeatedly awakens during the night, detachment parenting advises, "Let him cry one hour the first night, forty-five minutes the second night, and by the third night, he'll sleep through the night."

Parents, let me caution you. Difficult problems in child rearing do not have easy answers. Children are too valuable and their needs too important to be made victims of cheap, shallow advice. In my experience, parents who practice detachment parenting are at risk of losing their intuition and confidence and are less likely to achieve those two important goals of parenting, knowing their child and helping their child feel right.

## What's in It for Parents? The Payoff

What difference does the attachment style of parenting make? Will it make you a better parent? I have been sharing the above attachment tips with my patients over the last twenty-five years, and we have practiced them in our family. It does make a difference. Parents who practice the attachment style of parenting know their child well. They are observant of their infant's cues, respond to them intuitively, and are confident their responses are appropriate. They have realistic expectations of their child's behavior at various stages of development, and they know how to convey expected behavior to their child. Their children are a source of joy. The feeling that the attachment style of parenting gives you and your child can be summed up in one word: **harmony.**

Besides a harmonious relationship, the attachment style of parenting also promotes a **"hormoneous"** relationship. Mothers who practice these attachment tips actually undergo chemical changes. The hormone prolactin, often called the "mothering hormone," may enhance a woman's ability to mother as well as create a feeling of calmness and well-being during trying times. In experiments where this hormone is injected into male birds, they act like mothers. Mothers who practice the attachment style of parenting actually have more prolactin than mothers who exercise restraint. What makes the prolactin go up? You guessed it: unrestricted breastfeeding which naturally includes lots of skin-to-skin contact with the baby and sleeping with the baby. Science is finally catching up with what intuitive mothers have known all along: good things happen when mothers and babies spend more time with each other.

By now you may be thinking that attachment parenting is all giving, giving, giving. Well, to a certain extent, that is true. Mothers are givers and babies are takers—that is a realistic expectation of a mother-baby relationship. The baby's ability to give back will come later. Better takers usually become better givers. However, because of the hormone prolactin, as mothers give to babies, babies give something back to mothers. The attachment style of parenting allows mothering to stimulate more mothering.

## Why Attachment Parenting Works

Attachment parenting works because it respects the individual temperament of the child. The child comes equipped with a certain level of needs and the ability to give cues about what these needs are. The parents, by first being open to the child's cues, learn how to read the child and respond. Because the response helps the child feel right, he learns to cue better and parents learn to respond better. In a nutshell, both members of the parent-child communication network participate in the development of each other's skills. A cue-giving child and a responsive parent bring out the best in each other. On the other hand, detachment parenting with its restrained responses brings out the worst in both. The child's cries become more disturbing and parents become more angry. Baby and parent learn not to trust each other and eventually become insensitive to each other. Insensitivity gets parents into trouble.

The attachment style of parenting is especially effective when parenting the **high need child**. This little child goes by many well known names: the fussy baby, the difficult baby, the demanding baby, the challenging child, the strong-willed child. I prefer to call these children high need children. It is not only a more positive term, but it also describes the level of parenting these children need. These are the children who most need attachment parenting.

## What's in It for Your Child?

### Self-Esteem

The infant who is the product of attachment parenting learns that his needs will be met consistently and predictably. The child learns to trust. Trust creates the feeling that "I am a special person." This is the emergence of your child's self-esteem, the feeling of rightness which is so vitally important to the development of personality.

## Intimacy

The child learns to bond to persons, not things. The infant who is accustomed to being in arms, at breast, and in mommy and daddy's bed receives security and fulfillment from personal relationships. This infant is more likely to become a child who forms meaningful attachments with peers and in adulthood is more likely to develop a deep intimacy with a mate. The child who is often left by himself in swings, cribs, and playpens is at risk for developing shallow interpersonal relationships and becoming increasingly unfulfilled by a materialistic world.

## Nurturing Qualities

The child learns to be sensitive and giving. The child who receives the attachment style of parenting learns to care for others with the sensitive and giving quality that he received from his parents.

## Discipline

Practicing the attachment style of parenting actually makes discipline (that magic word you've all been waiting for) easier. Because you know your child better, you are able to read your child's behavior more accurately and respond more appropriately. Because your child feels right, he is more likely to act right. The child who has this inner feeling of rightness is more likely to develop a healthy conscience. He feels right when he does right and feels wrong when he does wrong. This style of parenting makes it easier to create an attitude within your child and an atmosphere within your home that makes punishment less necessary. When necessary, it is administered more appropriately. Because of their attachment to one another, parent and child trust each other. Trust is the basis of authority, and a trusted authority figure disciplines more effectively.

## Long-Term Benefits

Attachment parenting has long-term benefits, too. Let me share with you a very important concept of child-rearing called **modeling**: the parenting style children grow up with is the one they most likely will carry into their own parenting careers.

*Jim and Erin*

Remember, you are parenting someone else's future husband or future wife, and your grandchildren's future mother or father.

I will illustrate the importance of modeling by sharing with you two incidents which occurred in my practice and my family. One day a new mother brought her newborn baby into my office for a check-up. She also brought along her twenty-two-month-old daughter, Tiffany. When the newborn began to cry, Tiffany rushed to her mother and exclaimed, "Mommy, baby cry. Pick-up, rock-rock, nurse!"

Why had Tiffany responded so quickly to the cries of her sister? Because she had been modeled so. What will Tiffany do when she becomes a mother and her own baby cries? You guessed it! "Pick-up, rock-rock, nurse!".

The importance of modeling parenting styles to teenagers was driven home to my wife and me one day many years ago when we heard our nine-month-old daughter, Erin, crying from our bedroom. Since we believe in ministering promptly to our baby's cries, Martha and I started toward the bedroom. But then we heard the cries stop. As we approached the bedroom door we saw our fifteen-year-old, Jim, lying down on our bed next to Erin and gentling her and consoling her. Why did Jim do this? Jim had modeled his behavior after ours. He had learned that when babies cry someone listens and responds. As Martha and I witnessed this beautiful attachment scene we knew that both Erin and Jim felt right.

Jim is now a father himself, as is his older brother, Bob. As we watch these young men care for their own children and for their wives, our belief in the importance of modeling has been confirmed. We can't take all the credit for our sons' fine families, but we do know that how we have parented them and their siblings is making a difference in the next generation of the Sears family.

# Chapter 2

# How and Why Babies
# Sleep Differently Than Adults

Parents struggling with their child's sleeping habits need to know some general facts about sleep as well as specific facts about children's sleep. Children do sleep differently, and a basic understanding of what science has learned about sleep is necessary in order to appreciate the difference.

## States and Stages of Sleep

Sleep can be divided into two main states: active sleep and quiet sleep. Because the eyes move rapidly in active sleep, it is also called rapid eye movement or **REM sleep**. This is when dreaming takes place. The state in which the eyes are still is called **non-REM sleep**. REM sleep is also called light sleep, and non-REM, deep sleep, but **active sleep** and **quiet sleep** are more accurate terms.

Sleep progresses from a state of being awake through four stages of gradually deepening non-REM sleep. Stages three and four of non-REM sleep are the deepest sleep. This initial non-REM sleep period lasts from 90 to 110 minutes. Then the sleeper moves gradually back through the stages of non-REM sleep and enters the first period of REM sleep which lasts about 10 minutes. Then he goes back through the deepening states of sleep into another non-REM period. These cycles continue throughout the night, varying in length from 70 to 110 minutes (average 90 minutes). In the early part of the night non-REM sleep predominates. As the night progresses, the REM periods become progressively longer, as long as 60 minutes. Toward the waking hours the duration of REM and non-REM sleep is nearly the same. During an average eight-hour sleep, adults may spend approximately six hours in non-REM or quiet sleep and two hours in REM or active sleep.

## The Function of REM Sleep

Originally it was thought that REM sleep merely filled in the gaps between the periods of "real" non-REM sleep. However, more recent research has shown that periods of REM sleep have important functions.

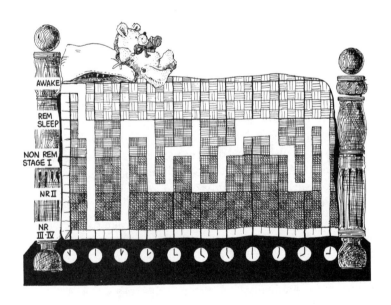

*During the night, sleepers move through several cycles of REM and non-REM sleep.*

There appears to be a physiological need for REM sleep. The two types of sleep are governed by different areas of the brain. Removing the part of the brain which governs REM sleep eventually leads to insomnia and death in experimental animals. If REM sleep is experimentally suppressed by drugs in newborn animals, they show sleep and brain dysfunctions as adults (Dement 1972). When a human being is deprived of sleep for several nights, the percentage of REM sleep increases dramatically during the catch-up nights.

Despite the appearance of being sound asleep, the brain is very much awake during the REM period. Sleep researchers describe REM sleep as mental exercise. The brain is engaged in dreaming, and upon awakening, the sleeper is able to recall this mental activity.

Tracing the development of sleep states through the levels of complexity in animals yields an understanding of the benefits of REM sleep. Simple animals have mostly non-REM sleep. In more complex animals, the brain is more developed and the percentage of REM sleep is greater. Is REM sleep the cause or the effect of a more developed brain? It would be easy to assume that REM sleep is a consequence of a more sophisticated brain, but prominent sleep researchers feel that it is the other way around. REM sleep may, in fact, be necessary for the brain to mature. This theory about REM sleep's influence on the developing brain has very interesting implications for understanding infant sleep patterns.

## REM Sleep and the Development of the Infant's Brain

In utero, the visual system receives much less stimulation than the other senses. Nevertheless, the visual tracks of the infant brain are well developed at birth. The fetus has a very high percentage of REM sleep. Some researchers believe that the REM state acts as **autostimulation** (self-stimulation) of the developing brain by providing visual imagery which promotes mental development (Roffwarg 1966). According to this theory, the lower brain centers fire off electrical impulses toward the higher brain centers. Reacting to these autostimuli helps the higher brain centers develop.

Observation of sleep patterns at different stages of life lends support to this theory. The younger the human being the greater the percentage of REM sleep. The early fetus may have nearly 100 percent REM sleep, the term infant around 50 percent, the two-year-old 25 percent, adolescents and adults 20 percent, and the elderly 15 percent. (See illustration below.) The period of life when humans sleep the most and the brain is developing rapidly is also when they require the most REM sleep. As the growing child receives more sensory stimulation from the outside environment, the need for stimulation from inside (the REM sleep state) lessens.

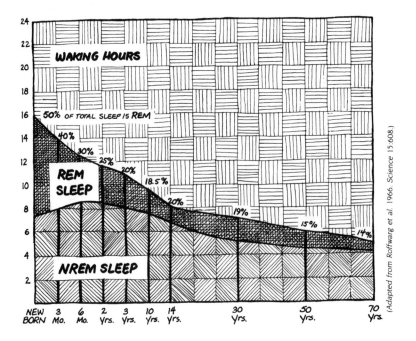

*As human beings mature, the need for REM sleep decreases.*

# "Doctor, My Baby Doesn't Sleep through the Night!"

Babies do, indeed, sleep differently, and tired parents need to have realistic expectations. After all, babies *don't* sleep through the night. Babies get their days and nights mixed up. Babies awaken frequently for feedings. Why? Because babies are designed that way. I want to share with you some insights into why babies sleep the way they do (or don't).

## Babies Need More REM Sleep Than Adults

Adults spend only 20 to 25 percent of their total sleep time in REM sleep and the rest (75 to 80 percent) in quiet or deep sleep. Adults have nearly twice as much quiet or non-REM sleep as tiny infants. Sleep in the infant from birth to three months occurs in the following proportions:

*45 to 50 percent of sleep time in REM sleep,*
*10 to 15 percent in transitional sleep,*
*35 to 45 percent in non-REM sleep.*

The high percentage of REM sleep in infancy gradually decreases to adult levels around two to three years of age.

When you watch your baby, you can tell when he is in the state of REM sleep. His eyes may be partially open, the eyeballs may move in unison, his breathing is irregular. He may exhibit facial twitches, grimaces, and smiles, and his body may be squirming around as he adjusts positions.

## Babies Spend More Time Moving from REM to Non-REM Sleep

In the first few months, not only does the infant have a larger percentage of REM sleep, but the four stages of non-REM sleep are not well developed. Thus much of a tiny infant's sleep occurs as transitional or indeterminate sleep. By three months of age, stages three and four of non-REM sleep are more defined.

### Babies Have Shorter Sleep Cycles Than Adults

A sleep cycle is the total time spent going through both the REM and non-REM states of sleep. Adults have sleep cycles lasting an average of ninety minutes, and REM sleep occurs an average of four times during the night. In infants the sleep cycle is shorter, and REM sleep occurs more frequently, every fifty to sixty minutes. An infant can have nearly twice as many REM periods in the same period of time as an adult. Because arousal (waking up) occurs more easily when emerging from the non-REM into the REM state of sleep, there are more vulnerable periods during the night when the infant may awaken.

### Babies Enter Sleep Differently than Adults

When adults fall asleep they go quickly into non-REM or quiet sleep without passing through an initial period of REM sleep. Adults can "crash" rather easily. Infants, on the other hand, routinely enter sleep through an initial period of REM sleep lasting around twenty minutes. They then enter a period of transitional sleep followed by quiet or non-REM sleep. If an arousal stimulus (such as a disturbing noise) occurs during this initial REM period or even during the transitional phase, the baby will reawaken easily because he has not yet reached the quiet sleep state. This accounts for the difficult-to-settle baby or the baby who has to be fully asleep before he can be put down. As babies mature, they become able to go from being awake directly into the state of quiet sleep without passing through a long period of active sleep. They settle quicker; they can be put down to go to sleep. The age at which babies go directly from waking to deep sleep varies from baby to baby. Studies have shown that some infants will enter sleep through a non-REM state by three months of age.

The fact that tiny infants enter sleep via the REM state suggests an important tip for nighttime parents. Infants should be **parented to sleep,** not just put down to sleep. Because the infant is more easily aroused from REM sleep, he needs to be gentled through the initial REM state until he descends into deep sleep. Likewise, if a baby rouses during a subsequent period of REM sleep, he can be gentled through it until he is again in a deep sleep.

### *Babies Have No Concept of Day and Night*

For adults, wakefulness is usually associated with day and sleep with night. They have been conditioned that way. The tiny infant does not begin to develop this conditioning until around three months, when more wakefulness begins to occur during the day and more sleep during the night. Nighttime parents need to organize their lifestyles and sleep patterns around their baby. For example, mothers are advised to nap during the day when their babies are sleeping.

## How the "Usual" Baby Develops Sleep Maturity and Begins to Settle

"Settling" means getting off to sleep easily and staying asleep, that is, sleeping through the night. The age at which babies settle and the number of hours of uninterrupted sleep they enjoy vary tremendously from baby to baby. In sleep studies settling is defined as sleeping through from midnight to 5:00 A.M. To expect a baby to sleep through the night from 8:00 P.M. to 8:00 A.M. is a totally unrealistic expectation for most babies. If you have a baby who sleeps long stretches at night consider this a luxury rather than a right.

In the first few months, most babies sleep fourteen to eighteen hours per day without any respect for the difference between day and night. A baby's sleep pattern resembles his feeding pattern: **small frequent feedings** and **short frequent naps.** Most newborns seldom sleep more than three to four hours at a stretch without awakening for a feeding. By four months of age, the total amount of sleep decreases very slightly, but the organization of sleep patterns improves. Babies are awake for longer stretches, and their sleep periods are longer and fewer. As their developing brains become capable of inhibiting arousal stimuli, the relative percentage of sleep gradually increases. By four months of age babies have usually developed some respect for waking during the day and sleeping at night. Initially the longest period of sleep may not be at night, but by three to four months most babies reward their parents with their longest period of sleep at night. In a study of a large group of infants, 70 percent of the babies settled (midnight to 5:00 A.M.) by three months, another 13 percent by six months (Moore 1957). Ten percent of the babies did not sleep uninterruptedly during the first year. Even among those infants who settled by six months of age, half continued to show periodic night-waking.

As babies get older, they approach sleep maturity. The total sleep time gradually decreases, the amount of active sleep decreases, quiet sleep increases, and the sleep cycles lengthen. This means fewer vulnerable periods in which babies may awaken. Settling seems to be a game of chance and playing percentages. If an **arousal stimulus** occurs during the vulnerable period of awakening, babies will wake up. If it occurs during the period of deeper sleep, babies are not likely to wake up. Some babies do not show improving sleep patterns because with increasing age the arousal stimuli may also increase: teething, colds, ear infections, and separation anxiety.

Although sleep patterns are more organized by one year of age, children from one to three may experience sleep problems because of emotional disturbances. Some children go to sleep easily and stay asleep. Some go to sleep with difficulty but stay asleep. Some go to sleep easily but do not stay asleep. Some exhausting children neither want to go to sleep nor stay asleep. Fears, separation anxieties, disturbing dreams, and nightmares are the main arousal stimuli from one to three years.

## Survival and Developmental Benefits

There are important reasons for the differences in sleep patterns between infants and adults. In the first few months the infant's needs are intense but his ability to communicate these needs is limited. Suppose babies had adult sleep patterns and enjoyed more deep sleep than light sleep. If they were hungry and needed food, they might not awaken. If they were cold and needed warmth, they might not awaken. If their noses were plugged and their breathing compromised, they might not awaken. I strongly feel that the infant's sleep pattern is "infantile" so that the infant can more easily communicate his or her survival needs.

Besides this survival benefit, the predominance of light sleep in tiny infants has **developmental benefits.** I mentioned earlier that light sleep is important for the development of the baby's brain. When your baby awakens during the night and you are tired and angry, appreciate that your baby is doing what he or she needs to be doing to grow and mature. One day in my office I explained all this to a mother of a wakeful baby. She listened thoughtfully and finally decided, "Well, in that case, my baby's going to be very smart."

**References**

Corner, M. A. 1980. Does REM sleep play a role in brain development? *Prog Brain Res* 53:347.

Dement, W. C. 1972. *Some Must Watch While Some Must Sleep.* San Francisco: W. H. Freeman and Co.

Freemon, F. R. 1972. *Sleep Research: A Critical Review.* Springfield, IL: Charles C. Thomas.

Moore, T. and Ucko, L. 1957. Night-waking in early infancy. *Arch Dis Child* 32:333.

Rahilly, P. M. 1980. The effects of sleep state and feeling on cranial blood flow of the human neonate. *Arch Dis Child* 55:265.

Roffwarg, F. R. et al. 1966. Ontogenetic development of the human sleep-dream cycle. *Science* 15:604.

# ━━━ *Chapter 3* ━━━
# Where Should Baby Sleep?

"Is it all right for the baby to sleep in our bed?"

This is a question I hear frequently from new parents. Let me say right at the outset that wherever all three of you (mother, father, and baby) sleep best and whatever leaves all of you feeling right is the best sleeping arrangement for your family. In my own family, we have practiced the concept of sharing sleep with our babies, a practice also known as the family bed, and I have advocated this co-sleeping arrangement to my patients. It works for most families most of the time. I am devoting most of this chapter to the concept of the family bed because I feel it is one of the most important parts of nighttime parenting. Actually, I prefer the term **sharing sleep** when discussing this concept. During the baby's first year, mother and child share more than bed space; they also share sleep patterns.

Sharing sleep may involve different arrangements for different families. It may mean having your baby sleep in your bed next to you or in a sidecar arrangement with his crib next to your bed. If your child is older, it may mean a mattress on the floor alongside your bed. For many families sharing sleep is a combination of all these arrangements.

Sharing sleep involves more than a decision about where your baby sleeps. It reflects an attitude of acceptance of your child as a little person with big needs. Your infant trusts that you, his parents, will be continually available during the night just as you are during the day. Sharing sleep also requires that you trust your intuition about the parenting of your individual child rather than unquestioningly accepting the norms of society. Acceptance of your baby's needs can help you recognize that you are not spoiling your baby or letting him manipulate your household when you allow him to sleep with you.

### Sharing Sleep Develops Mother's Intuition

*One mother described her progress toward sleep harmony in a letter she wrote to me:*

After the birth of my first baby I went through an experience that I was in no way prepared for: postpartum depression. The tension and stress I felt from suddenly becoming a new mother caused me to actually be scared of my baby at times. Compounding my tension was the thought that since I'd be returning to work soon, I felt like I would be abandoning my baby.

All of these doubts and uncertainties manifested themselves in a bout of insomnia that stretched for four days. I'd lay my baby in her crib at night, then go to my room and just pray that I would get some sleep before she woke up for the next feeding. This was a mistake. While I tried to force myself to relax I was aware of every turn, gurgle, and sigh that she was making in the next room.

By the time I called you I was desperate for help. You suggested that I bring her into bed with me at night. I tried it, and although I was slightly nervous at first, afraid I would roll onto her, I quickly found that I was able to sleep and relax when she was next to me.

I think that having a family bed has brought us closer together as mother and daughter. Spending the night together, holding her and then breastfeeding her when she wakes up, has made me feel more confident about mothering her during the day. Besides, as my husband says, what better way to start the day than to wake up and see both your lover and your child lying next to you.

# Advantages of Sharing Sleep

## *Babies Sleep Better*

Sharing sleep helps babies organize their sleep patterns. The last chapter discussed how babies have vulnerable periods for waking up as they pass from deep or quiet sleep into light or active sleep. These vulnerable periods occur as often as once every hour during the night. Sleeping with a familiar and predictable person smooths the passage from one sleep state to the next and lessens the baby's anxiety. When a baby awakens partially during these vulnerable periods, the attachment person helps him resettle himself before he is fully awake. For older children **attachment objects** such as a favorite doll, a teddy bear, or a ragged old blanket help smooth the transition from one sleep state to the next. A tiny baby, however, needs an **attachment person,** usually mother.

To a tiny baby, when mother is out of sight she ceases to exist. The baby has not yet developed **object permanence**. If he awakens and mother is not there, he does not yet possess the cognitive ability to realize, "She's just around the corner in another room." Babies usually do not achieve object permanence until some time after the first year. Providing a familiar attachment person during the night helps a baby feel certain that mother has not left.

A newborn has already been sleeping in touch with his mother for nine months. He has grown accustomed to the presence of familiar breathing movements, a heartbeat, and warmth. The fact that the baby has been "all of a sudden born" doesn't mean this should change.

I remember awakening in the morning and gazing upon the contented face of our nine-month-old "sleeping beauty." I could tell when she was ascending from her level of deep sleep to light sleep. As she passed through the vulnerable period of awakening she often reached out for her mother or me. When she touched one of us, an "I'm okay" expression would radiate from her face, her eyes would remain closed, and she would not awaken. However she often awakened if she reached out and one of us was not within touching distance.

### Mothers Sleep Better

This may come as a surprise, but not only does baby sleep better in the family bed, most parents do also. Certainly mother usually does. Baby is not the only one who is separation sensitive at night. A new mother also experiences anxiety when her baby is not nearby. She lies awake and wonders, "Is my baby all right?" The farther away she is from her baby the deeper this anxiety.

Achieving harmony with your baby during the day is an important part of attachment parenting. Sharing sleep allows this harmony to continue. Physical closeness causes mother and baby to share sleep cycles; their internal clocks are synchronized with each other. When baby wakes during a vulnerable period, mother is likely to be in light sleep. She can help the baby settle again without her sleep cycles being seriously disrupted. It may take a little while to master sleep

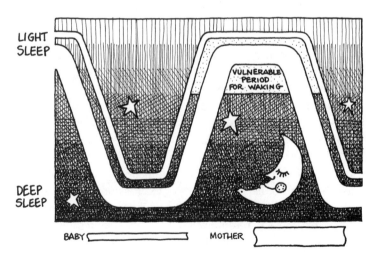

*The breastfeeding mother and baby have similar sleep cycles.*

# Why Doesn't My Baby Sleep Through the Night?

*"Our three-month-old baby has never slept through the night. I was not worried at first because I figured she would sleep through by three months when the book said she should. She goes to bed easily around eight o'clock, but after that, it's all over. She awakens every two hours. I go into her room, nurse her, put her back down, and sometimes she awakens again within a few minutes or an hour or two later. I am up and down all night like a yo-yo. My husband moves to another room to sleep on the couch, and our marriage is being affected, at least at night. My friends' babies are sleeping through the night by now. Am I doing something wrong?"*

It is true that many babies organize their sleep patterns around the third or fourth month and begin rewarding their parents with longer stretches of sleep at night. You have a baby who has not been able to organize her sleep patterns by the usual age. It is nothing that you are doing wrong, and you will never know why she has not been able to sleep alone. The question is not why she has the problem, but what you're going to do about it. Your baby is giving you a clear message: "I can't sleep alone." Take your baby into your bed. Either put her into your bed when she first goes down to sleep at night or after she wakes up for the first time. By sleeping with your baby and alleviating her anxiety, you and your baby will get your sleep cycles synchronized with each other. Your baby probably will wake up less often, and she will eventually learn to wake up during your lighter sleep rather than waking you from a state of deep sleep which is what really interferes with your rest. If your baby continues to nurse frequently at night, you will find that many times you may not even completely awaken during a feeding. It may take the whole family several weeks to adjust to this new arrangement. Solving the problem is more difficult than preventing it.

harmony, but mothers who have achieved this synchronization report that they do feel rested. Mothers must first learn to sleep like babies in order to help their babies learn to sleep like adults.

When harmony in sleep is not achieved, nighttime parenting becomes a reluctant duty. Being awakened from a state of deep sleep to attend to a hungry and crying baby makes the concept of nighttime parenting unattractive and leads to exhausted mothers, fathers, and babies.

## Breastfeeding Is Easier

When mother's and baby's sleep cycles are in harmony, night nursing is less tiring. Mothers usually find it much easier to roll over and nurse than to get out of bed, go into another room, turn on a light, pick up a crying baby, locate a rocking chair, and finally feed the baby. By this time both mother and baby are wide awake. Family bed nursing meets the needs of the nursing couple without either one becoming fully awake.

The harmony between the nursing mother and the sucking infant who sleep together is illustrated by the experiences that mothers often share with me. They find that their sleep lightens and they almost wake up about thirty seconds before their babies awaken for a feeding. By being able to anticipate the

---

## *The Lazy Mom Option*

We have three children, and I like my sleep at night. So we adopted a sleeping arrangement I call the Lazy Mom Option. The more easily I could meet my baby's nighttime needs and get back to sleep the better. So the baby slept in bed with us. That way I could get to him quicker and nurse him before he became revved up into a full-blown cry. In this way, he resettled faster and so did I. When he became an older baby (and a squirmer) we placed a mattress on the floor beside our bed. I would nurse him to sleep on this mattress, and when he awakened during the night I would simply crawl down, nurse him, and crawl back into bed.

feeding, mothers usually start nursing just as the baby begins to squirm and reach for the nipple. The babies do not fully awaken and drift back into deep sleep right after nursing.

### Prolactin Levels Increase

Prolactin has been called the "mothering" hormone and is perhaps the chemical basis for mothers' intuition. Prolactin levels go up in response to nipple stimulation. They also increase during sleep and when a person is under stress. Increased prolactin levels may help a breastfeeding mother feel calmer and more accepting of her baby's demands, day and night. Nursing the baby while sharing naps and nighttime sleep releases prolactin which counteracts the stress of caring for baby's needs. Mothering stimulates more mothering as long as you let it happen.

I have noticed a very interesting phenomenon which occurs in mothers who sleep with their babies, especially mothers of high need babies. These mothers often tell me that as time goes on they seem to need less sleep and feel more rested despite the fact that their babies continue to awaken and nurse frequently during the night. Mothers' acceptance and tolerance level seems to increase. I wonder if increased prolactin (which I also call a perseverance hormone) could be responsible for the increasing tolerance for nighttime parenting. Increased prolactin levels may help you achieve sleep harmony.

### Sharing Sleep Increases Touching

The skin is the largest organ in the human body, and tactile stimulation or the lack of it can have a profound effect on how the baby develops. Dr. Ashley Montagu, in his book *Touching: The Human Significance of the Skin* (1978), makes a convincing argument that tactile stimulation is beneficial to the entire baby, physically,

**Peaceful Nights**

I have just had my third child and now I fully realize how great the family bed is and how much easier it is to get a lot of sleep with the baby in bed with you. When he was only three hours old, I brought him in bed with me. He slept five hours straight. I only slept two of those hours because I was so high from giving birth I just stared at him for three hours. The skin-to-skin contact really mellowed him, and he was so relaxed he slept soundly. We continued this arrangement, and he is now six weeks old. He always has a period of sleep that lasts five or six hours. He never cries at night because I hear him stirring which means he is waking up. So his needs at night are met immediately. If he gets restless during the night, I put my hand on his stomach, and he relaxes and goes back to sleep.

My grandmother had ten children, and I learned recently that when a new baby was born, my grandmother slept with the new baby and my grandfather slept in another bed with the former baby.

emotionally, and intellectually. The extra touching that a baby receives by sleeping with his parents definitely has a beneficial effect on his development. I suspect that infants who sleep with their mothers grow better. One of the oldest treatments for the slow-gaining baby is to tell the mother, "Take your baby to bed and nurse." How much of the growth that results is due to extra nourishment and how much is due to extra touching is difficult to determine. I suspect that babies thrive better when sleeping with their parents because of a combination of both nutritional and sensory inputs.

### Children Sleep Better

In my survey on sleep problems most parents reported that their children slept better when sharing sleep. They awakened less often and experienced fewer nightmares and nighttime disturbances. Co-sleeping helps children develop a healthy

## Rattling the Cage

*"Several times during the night our two-year-old awakens us. When I go into his room he is standing up in his crib rattling the sides. Some nights he has even managed to climb over the bars and down onto the floor. I can't put him back into his crib without a severe protest that gets both of us angry and wide awake."*

If you are open to your child's cues, you will see that he is rattling his crib because he does not like being caged in. Either he does not want to be in a cage, or he does not want to be alone. At the risk of sounding ridiculous, you have two choices in this situation: either sleep in his cage with him (but to my knowledge nobody manufactures king-size cribs) or adopt an alternative sleeping arrangement which gets your child out of his crib.

Some two-year-olds are ready for their own beds, but if you feel that your child is too restless and may fall out of bed, simply put a mattress on the floor so that if he rolls off he will not hurt himself. If a change to his own bed does not work, your child may really be asking to sleep close to you. In this case, welcome him into your bed, put his mattress next to your bed, or move his crib into your room. Whichever works and gets all of you—parents and child—the most sleep is the right sleeping arrangement for your family.

Some advisors might actually tell you that if your child won't stay in his crib, you should put a net over it so that he can't get out. Do not follow this advice. This makes your child's cage even more fearful and hateful, and you're not getting to the root of the problem. Insisting that your child stay in a crib when he is giving you clear messages that he can't sleep there alone usually results in an unending nighttime power struggle which nobody wins. For a moment, put yourself in your child's place. Would you like to wake up in a dark, lonely room surrounded on all sides by bars and covered by an escape-proof net?

sleep attitude. They learn to regard sleep as a pleasant time, a time of closeness. They radiate a feeling of rightness because the principles of daytime attachment parenting are carried over into nighttime parenting. Children who sleep alone (especially if they don't want to sleep alone) often grow up regarding sleep as a fearful time, a time of separation. One mother told me that she still suffers from frequent nightmares and always remembers her fear of sleep as a child. For this reason she welcomed her child into her bed so that "she wouldn't grow up like me, being afraid of sleep."

It is not abnormal or unusual for older children to sleep with their parents, just "uncultural." A mother I know told me, "When our five-year-old comes in and wants to spend the night with us, we regard it as a stress indicator and we open our bedroom to him." It is common and quite normal for children occasionally to pop into the parents' bedroom for some refueling and nighttime security.

Welcoming your child into the family bed or bedroom (instead of merely allowing it) tells him, "You are a special person. We care about you at night just as we care about you during the day." Therefore, sharing sleep encourages a feeling of rightness within your child. A child who feels right inside is more likely to act right on the outside. Sharing sleep is particularly beneficial if you and your child have one of those days when you "locked horns" and neither of you was able to get through to the other. Parenting your child to bed and welcoming your child into your bed help to end the day on a good note.

### Fathers Benefit Too

This may come as a surprise to many fathers, but even fathers profit from sleeping with their babies. Once they get used to it, many fathers report to me that they feel closer to their babies. Fathers' feelings about nighttime parenting are discussed in detail in Chapter Nine.

━━━━━━━ *Asleep on the Doorstep* ━━━━━━━

*"Sometimes when we get up in the morning, we find our two-year-old asleep on the floor outside our bedroom door."*

The answer is simple: Open your door and let your child in. Children usually achieve object permanence by eighteen months of age. Even though they cannot see their parents, they know they exist and they know how to find them. In this situation, your child is giving you a clear message that he does not want to or cannot sleep alone, but he is not persistent enough to come storming into your room in the middle of the night. Take the not-so-subtle cue from your child that he wants to sleep in your room.

## Child Spacing Comes Naturally

I once mentioned to a father of a large family that when mothers and babies sleep together, children are usually spaced further apart. "Of course," he responded, "mother is too tired to do anything but sleep." This is not the real reason sharing sleep spaces babies. Most studies show that breastfeeding is a natural contraceptive in approximately 98 percent of mothers for the first six months postpartum, as long as the rules of the game are followed. The rules state that breastfeeding is an effective means of contraception as long as a mother can answer "no" to the following questions:

1. *Have your menses returned?*
2. *Are you supplementing regularly or allowing long periods without breastfeeding, either during the day (more than four hours) or at night (more than six hours)?*
3. *Is your baby more than six months old?*

Note the importance of nursing at night in maintaining a woman's infertility. Night nursing is most effective as a contraceptive when babies and mothers sleep together, and mothers who sleep with their babies and nurse them often during the night can usually look forward to more than six months of infertility. See Chapter Ten for more on breastfeeding's contraceptive effect.

### Sharing Sleep Has Long-Term Effects

Is sleeping with my baby going to help him become a brighter and happier child? There are many variables that contribute to children's growth and development. However, psychologists agree that the quantity and quality of mothering does affect the emotional and intellectual development of the child. Extending the practice of daytime attachment parenting into nighttime parenting does have long-term effects on the child.

One of these effects is on the quality of intimacy. Many psychologists and marriage counselors report that one of the common problems of contemporary teenagers and adults is that they have difficulty forming genuinely close and intimate relationships with another person. Teddy bears and baby bottles have helped us raise a generation of people attached primarily to material things. Sharing sleep teaches a child to be

## Sleep Memories

*An East African tribal chief who was eighty years old spoke these words:*

My early years are connected in my mind with my mother. At first she was always there; I can remember that comforting feel of her body as she carried me on her back and the smell of her skin in the hot sun. Everything came from her. When I was hungry or thirsty she would swing me around to where I could reach her full breasts. Now when I shut my eyes, I feel again with gratitude the sense of well-being that I had when I buried my head in their soft nest and drank the sweet milk that they gave. At night when there was no sun to warm me, her arms, her body, took its place, and as I grew older and more interested in other things, from my safe place on her back I could watch without fear, and when sleep over-came me I had only to close my eyes (Montagu 1978).

comfortable being in touch with somebody; it doesn't substitute things for people. A childhood need for intimacy that is not filled never completely goes away but reappears in later years. Psychologists report that many adult fears and sleep problems can be traced back to uncorrected sleep disturbances during childhood.

### Thanks for the Memories

One of the most precious gifts you can give your child is a vivid memory of happy childhood attachments. What a beautiful memory it is for a child to recall how he was parented to sleep in the arms of his father or mother or to recall how he awakened in the morning surrounded on all sides by people he loves rather than in a lonely room in a wooden cage peering out through bars. I remember how happy our children were when they awoke in our bed. I would look over at the baby sleeping next to me and see a contented look on her face that said, "Thanks, Mom and Dad, for having me here." Memories last a lifetime.

## Why Parents Hesitate

Despite the advantages, some parents hesitate to adopt sharing sleep as part of their parenting style. If you're a parent with doubts, perhaps the following information will alleviate your concerns.

### Cultural Programming

Isn't sleeping with a baby an unusual custom? What will people say? Actually just the opposite is true. Babies sleeping with parents is the usual custom in most cultures around the world. Co-sleeping was common in the Western world until the twentieth century when mothers lost confidence in their own instincts and followed the advice of a few influential but misguided experts. Even today mothers sleep with their babies but are afraid to tell their doctors or in-laws about it.

If you want to get a feeling for how prevalent sharing sleep really is, walk up to a group of young mothers and confide to one of them, "My baby sleeps with me." Your confidante will probably look around to make sure that no one else is listening and will whisper back to you, "My baby does, too, but don't tell anybody."

These mothers are doing what their instincts tell them to do, but because of ridiculous social taboos, they are made to feel uneasy about it. In taking a poll of mothers I have tried to pin down the ambivalent ones as to what their real feelings are toward sleeping with their babies. Most mothers will admit, "Deep down inside I feel it is right, but because so many people tell me not to, I feel uneasy."

Well, mothers you can now relax. There is safety in numbers. In my own survey, three out of four mothers favored sleeping with their babies. In the years since this book was first published, the concept of sharing sleep has grown in popularity (or maybe parents have just become more comfortable admitting that their babies sleep with them). In one study of two- and three-year-old children, most of the parents reported that their child slept in their bed at least occasionally and for at least part of the night (Madansky and Edelbrock 1990). It is not true that the attachment style of parenting is practiced only by fringe groups or fanatics. In fact, studies show breastfeeding rates as high as 80 percent among more educated mothers from higher socio-economic groups, and breastfeeding mothers are the group most likely to be sleeping with their babies.

### Doctor's Advice

Another stumbling block is professional advice. "But my doctor told me not to let our baby sleep in our bed." Parents should not have to ask the doctor for permission to let their child sleep with them, and the doctor should not be giving parents a definite yes or no answer. This type of advice is a carryover from the days when new mothers felt more comfortable taking the advice of the doctor than following their own instincts. Mothers put doctors on the spot when they ask them where their babies should sleep. Doctors are trained in the diagnosis and treatment of illnesses, not in parenting styles. Where baby should sleep is not a medical question requiring a medical decision. Fortunately doctors are becoming more flexible and less authoritarian. Be sure to choose doctors who are comfortable with your parenting style. When it comes to mother-infant attachment your instincts should be followed above the advice of anyone else. The other person has no biological attachment to your infant.

Many new mothers do feel a bit shaky in following their own intuition. As one mother said to me, "I don't feel I have any instinct." One of the reasons for today's mothers' lack of confidence is that they often have no models of attachment parenting to follow either in their own parents or among their peers. If you need advice concerning parenting styles, ask an experienced mother. In my opinion, you will generally receive the best advice from mothers in the breastfeeding and mothering organization, La Leche League International.

## *Dependency*

How often have you heard "But the baby will get to enjoy it, he'll become so dependent that he'll never want to leave your bed"? Yes, of course, the baby will enjoy it. Is there anything in the parent-child contract that says your baby shouldn't enjoy where he sleeps? Yes, he will temporarily seem dependent and not want to leave your bed. This is a natural consequence of the feeling of rightness. When you're close to someone you love and you feel right, why give that up?

You are not encouraging dependency when you sleep with your baby. You are responding to a need and teaching your child about trust. Your child will not grow up to be less independent because he slept in your bed. In my experience, children who are given open access to the family bed in infancy become more secure and independent in the long run. They reach the stage of independence when they are ready. Independence is not, in itself, one of our most important parenting goals. It is not the parents' responsibility to make a child independent but rather to create a secure environment and a feeling of rightness which allows a child's independence to develop naturally.

This gets back to the concept of weaning as discussed earlier. Timely weaning—whether from the breast or from the parents' bed—brings fulfillment, not dependency. Sleeping close to or with the parents is part of a natural continuum from

## Testimony from Tired Parents

The night I came home from the hospital I just couldn't put my tiny helpless little baby in her new crib to sleep. Instead her father and I took her into the security and warmth of our own bed. When the baby cried I always picked her up and nursed her so that she would be content. It got so that she seemed to nurse continually day and night, but I didn't mind because it satisfied me to be close and able to meet her every helpless need.

Many people comment to my husband and me how happy and content our baby seems to be all the time. I really believe that this is due, in part, to two basic factors: nursing on demand and having her sleep in our bed.

I was ambivalent about sleeping with my baby until my pediatrician said, "Do what you feel is right." This released me and I started to enjoy sleeping with my baby.

mother's womb to mother's breast to mother's bed. A child who is weaned from any of these places of security before he is ready is at risk of exhibiting undesirable behaviors of premature weaning. These behaviors, which I call "diseases of unreadiness," include aggressive behavior, anger, tantrums, depression, and negativism. It is important that you allow your child to mature on the terms that feel right for both of you and not according to a preconceived time chart set by outside pressure from childcare providers.

"But when will he leave our bed?" In the important relationships with your children, throw away the clock and the calendar. Do not put time limits on these beautiful relationships. The main issue is not when your child leaves your bed, but how he leaves. If you don't set a deadline, you won't have unfulfilled expectations. My general experience both in my practice and in my family is that most children who are welcomed into the family bed in early infancy voluntarily leave around the second or third year. They may return periodically in times of stress or high need. Remember, a need that is filled does go away. It may last a little longer than we expect, but eventually it will pass. There may be a gradual weaning period.

Instead of going directly from your bed to his own room, your child may sleep for a while on his own mattress or in a sleeping bag on the floor alongside your bed or in a sibling's room.

The age at which children are weaned from the family bed depends on several factors including the parents' desire to "ship them out" and how sensitive they are to separation. Some high need children are very sensitive to separation and may not be too quick to give up the security of the family bed. For example, one of the high need children in my practice did not wean herself from mother's breast and her parents' bed until she was four years old. Now at age six, she is a very secure, independent, and giving child.

## Overlaying

Some mothers are afraid that they might roll over on the baby and smother him. In times gone by, the death of an infant during sleep was often attributed to overlaying by the mother or wet nurse. Mothers that I have interviewed on this subject have told me that they are so physically and mentally aware of their baby's presence even when sleeping that it is extremely unlikely they would overlay their baby.

Some parents fear that father might roll over on the baby or fling an arm out and hurt the baby. Fathers usually are less aware of the presence of a baby in bed than mothers. Having the baby sleep between mother and a guard rail or a wall can alleviate these fears.

There are still occasional reports of infant death allegedly caused by overlaying, but these are very difficult to substantiate. During a speaking tour some years ago I visited New Zealand, where because of the medical reporting system, authorities are able to obtain very good records on the causes of infant death. I had the opportunity to talk with one of the local pediatricians concerning several cases of infant death which had been attributed to overlaying. In each of these cases there seemed to be an unusual family sleeping situation. The parents were intoxicated, or there were many children in one small bed and an older child overlaid the tiny baby. While overlaying does happen, it is rare and is almost always due to unsafe sleep practices. I concluded that the fear of overlaying should not keep families from enjoying the concept of sharing sleep. It would, however, be unwise to sleep with a baby if mother or father's awareness is diminished by alcohol or other drugs. (See the next section fpr more information for safe sleep-sharing.)

It is interesting that the fear of Suden Infant Death Syndrome (SIDS) is occasionally given as one of the reasons why mothers sleep with their babies. A mother who chose to sleep with her baby told me that if her infant was struggling to breathe, she would want to be by his side. If he did die by her side, she would be reassured that she had done everything possible to save him. If her baby died in another room, she thought she would always have the feeling, "I was not there when my baby needed me, and I may have been able to save his life." Sharing sleep may lessen the chance of SIDS. For more on this, see Chapter Twelve.

### Tips for Safe Sleep-Sharing.

A few precautions will help you share sleep safely with your baby. Consider the following:

*Use a guard rail or push the bed flush against the wall, and position baby between mother and the wall, rather than between the parents. Mothers are usually more physically and mentally aware of the baby's presence than fathers.*

*If you use a guard rail, be sure that it is held flush against the side of the mattress, so that there is no crevice into which baby might slip. Plastic mesh guard rails are safer than those with slats, which can entrap an arm, a leg, or even baby's head.*

*If you push your bed against a wall, be sure there is no space between the mattress and the wall to entrap baby. With some kinds of beds, the bedframe may be touching the wall, but the mattress is not. Younger babies can slip into the crack between the mattress and the wall and suffocate.*

*Use a large bed, preferably a king-size. It is not safe for babies to sleep with too many sleepers in too small a bed. Do not let older siblings sleep with a tiny baby. Children do not have the same awareness of a sleeping baby that parents do.*

*Do not fall asleep with a baby on a couch. The baby may become wedged between your body and the back of the couch, or his head could get buried in cushions or crevices between cushions.*

*Do not sleep with baby on a free-floating, wavy water bed. The baby's face can become trapped in the depression made by his head or body, or by a parent's body. His neck muscles aren't strong enough to lift his head out of this sinking surface. Crevices between the mattress and the frame are also a hazard, even on "waveless" water beds. Be sure these are filled in.*

*Do not sleep with your baby if you are under the influence of alcohol or any other drug (such as a tranquilizer) that diminishes your awareness of your baby's presence. Alcohol and some medications alter sleep cycles and affect your ability to arouse from sleep.*

*Don't wear lingerie with string ties longer than 7 inches (17.5 centimeters). Babies can strangle in strings. Avoid dangling jewelry as well.*

*Be aware of overheating. Because of the closeness of warm bodies, a baby who is sleeping with parents probably does not need to be dressed as warmly at night as a baby who is sleeping alone.*

These safety tips are not here to frighten you or to make sleep-sharing seem difficult but to help you ensure that baby and you enjoy a safe, comfortable and worry-free sleeping environment.

### Sexuality and Sexual Relations

"Allowing our baby in our bed might ruin our sex life."

The fears about this are unwarranted. I don't believe that the love between parents can adversely affect the product of their love. Embracing and showing affection between husband and wife are healthy in front of children of any age.

Parents' main concern is about genital foreplay and sexual intercourse. Since tiny babies have a limited awareness and understanding of what's going on anyway, lovemaking in the family bed is seldom a problem when your infant is only a few months old. As the baby gets older parents seldom feel comfortable enjoying lovemaking in the presence of a sleeping child. Couples who have successfully employed the concept of the family bed have discovered that the master bedroom is not the only place for lovemaking and that every room in the house becomes a potential love chamber. This may lead to more creativity in the couple's sexual relationship. Another option is to move the sleeping child into another room.

========= *Parents' Nighttime Needs* =========

*"The only way my baby and I could get any sleep was
to sleep together. We nursed without either of us fully
awakening. My husband, however, was too sensitive to
the baby's noises and couldn't sleep with her in our
bed. So he slept on the family room couch.*

*"We both had nighttime needs, too. Very frequently
when I was awake I would go into the family room and
join my husband for some special time together."*

I wonder what that husband might have felt the first
night his wife greeted him with this nighttime surprise.
It is rather unusual for a new mother to initiate lovemaking, and I'm sure this helped dad better accept the family
room couch.

It has often been said that "a baby should not come
between a husband and wife, in bed or otherwise." As a father
of eight, who has practiced the concept of sharing sleep, I can
say that our babies have not come between my wife and me.
The attachment style of parenting works best in the context of
a fulfilled marriage. It is absolutely necessary that husband and
wife find their private time alone.

I feel it is healthy for the child to get two messages
concerning the parents' bedroom: The door is open to me if
I have a strong need to be with my parents, but there are
private times when mommy and daddy need to be alone.

You can kindly but firmly request that an older, verbal child
leave your bedroom and "go watch cartoons" because mommy
and daddy are loving. A child who is not able to handle this
probably has a history of being shut out, put off, or rejected
frequently, problems much deeper than the issue of parental
privacy.

Whatever your viewpoints on how much show of affection
should occur in front of your child, consider the fact that,
whatever the cause, the current system is certainly not
working. Many teenagers and young adults are having problems
with sexual identity. Real intimacy is difficult for many young
couples, and there is an increasing demand for sexual

counseling. How many of the sexual problems of today result from the lack of family intimacy that was so prevalent a few decades ago? Now that family co-sleeping is on the increase will there be fewer sexual problems in the next generation?

## Reasons Why Sleeping with Your Baby Appears Not to Work

In my experience, if the concept of sharing sleep is practiced with an accepting attitude, it works for most parents most of the time. There are times, however, when sleeping with the baby does not seem to work for some families. Many of these problems, however, can be solved or avoided.

### It's Started Late

Parents may wait to try sharing sleep until difficult sleep problems have already occurred. Having tried everything else, they reluctantly, as the last resort, admit defeat and allow their baby into their bed, but down deep they don't want him there. Neither baby nor parent is accustomed to this sleeping arrangement, and a harmony of sleep cycles has not been established. Babies seem to sense these negative vibrations, and neither parents nor baby settle well. What should be a beautiful, positive family experience becomes a negative one.

━━━━━━━━━━ *Surviving the Squirmer* ━━━━━━━━━━

*"We have welcomed our two-year-old into our bed at night, but he squirms so much nobody sleeps."*

A child who has not been accustomed to sleeping with someone has not yet learned to respect the other person's sleeping space. Try sleeping in the "teddy bear snuggle"; cuddling may help him settle down. Or try the hands-on approach. Firmly place your hand or arm on the squirming sleeping child and hold him in place until he gets the message and settles. Your squirmer can also be placed on his mattress next to your bed or somewhere in your bedroom. You can easily go to his mattress when he needs you.

*A big bed and a guard rail make sharing sleep more
comfortable for everyone in the family.*

In general, correcting a problem takes more effort than
prevention. For families who are starting to share sleep as a
solution to problems, it may take longer to achieve nighttime
harmony. This is one of the reasons why I suggest that couples
welcome the baby into their bed very early in infancy,
preferably in the newborn period. This will get your sleep
cycles in harmony so that sleep problems can either be
prevented or minimized.

### "I'm Too Aware of Him"

Some mothers have told me, "Our baby is one of those
squirmers. She is all over the bed, and no one gets any sleep."
Others relate, "I've tried sleeping with my baby, but I am too
aware of every little noise and movement she makes and I can't
sleep." These problems can be the result of starting the family
bed later when harmony has not been established from birth.
Give yourself a few weeks of trying shared sleep, and you
probably will no longer awaken at every little noise. Older
babies can be told to respect the sleeping space of other
members in the family bed. Some children are little "rock-and-
rollers" at night, especially if they haven't become accustomed
to co-sleeping. A possible solution is to have an extended bed

## Compulsion Gives Way to Acceptance

The family bed—I resisted this one! After finally getting
the baby to bed, I strongly needed my own space especially in the hot weather when I can't stand to sleep near
another hot sweaty body. But as a last resort, I was will-
ing. I put the baby in the middle, and I positioned myself
on the very edge of the bed with my nightstand and a
chair full of pillows strategically placed to keep me from
falling out of bed. I told my husband to keep as close to
his edge as possible because he had an extra one hundred
pounds on his side and the baby would roll downhill
against his body if he were too close to us. Then I would
have to retrieve him before I could nurse him when he
woke up. I forgot to take into consideration that the baby
also requires a lot of sleeping space. He tosses and turns
worse than I do. Every time he rolled into us, he'd wake
up. It was worse than before. After a week of this, we
were back to square one.

Well, experience is certainly the best teacher and
after enough experience, I finally found my solution. I
simply accepted the fact that there is no solution. Our
baby isn't a robot that can be programmed, any more
than we are. Now I no longer plan my strategy each
night. Just as his pattern varies, so does mine.
Sometimes I get up and sit in the rocker and nurse him
back to sleep while I relax and doze. Sometimes I'm too
tired to sit up, and I bring him to bed where he spends
the rest of the night. I don't worry anymore about being
strategically positioned. I let the baby roll into my husband. It gives me more room and Daddy gets a kick out
of waking up and finding a baby in his armpit.

onto which the baby can be moved so his squirming is less likely
to bother anyone.

One very accepting husband told me that quite often he
and his wife awaken in the morning with their one-year-old
stretched out between them with his head on Mommy and his
feet on Daddy, in an "H" position. It's as though the baby wants
to keep in touch with both persons he loves.

━━━━━━━ *Making Room for a New Baby* ━━━━━━━

*"I am expecting a baby in a month and our three-year-old is still sleeping with us. I don't want to exile him from our bed, but I honestly feel I can't handle two kids at night."*

If you don't relish having both your three-year-old and your new baby in your bed, there are alternatives. (Admittedly, more than one child in your bed may not work unless your bedroom has a wall-to-wall mattress.) The problem is how to persuade your three-year-old to accept an alternative without his feeling banished from his nighttime place of security. Remember, weaning a child from your bed means you must substitute alternative forms of comfort and nourishment. As you mother your newborn at night ask your husband to father the three-year-old. Treat this as something special: "Daddy and you are going to sleep together on a big mattress (or in your own room)." The three-year-old will probably feel that though he has lost a bit of mommy, he has gained more of daddy with no overall net loss

━━━━━━━━━━━━━━━━━━━━━━━━━━━━━━━━

### Father Doesn't Sleep Well with Baby in the Bed
Most fathers are actually disturbed less than mother at night because mother is the food source. However, the sleep cycle harmony between mothers and babies does not exist between babies and fathers, so that fathers are more likely to be awakened from a state of deep sleep. This can be minimized by letting the baby sleep between mother and an adjacent guard rail or wall rather than between mother and father.

### The Bed Is Too Small
Sharing sleep seldom works if your bed is smaller than queen-size. Each family member needs enough space. A king-size bed will probably be your most useful piece of baby furniture. The money you would save by not buying a crib could be used to buy a larger bed. If a king-size bed is not possible, your present bed can be extended by the sidecar arrangement described below.

### Parents Honestly Don't Want Their Baby in Their Bed

This concern was shared with me one day by a very caring and committed mother of a large family. She said, "By bedtime I've had enough of kids. This is my special time with my husband and I simply don't want our baby in our bed." I certainly supported this mother's feelings. She honestly felt that for her particular family situation it was necessary that she have this special time with her husband (and herself) at night to nurture the marriage and recharge her own batteries so that she could be a more effective mother by day. This was not a selfish decision but a realistic appraisal that the whole family would probably function better if they had separate sleeping arrangements. This mother has realistic expectations of her own tolerance level, and she is blessed with children who apparently are not separation sensitive.

### Mother and Father Don't Agree on Sleeping Arrangements

Occasionally a mother will complain, "I want my babies to sleep next to me, but my husband refuses." In my experience, the family bed seldom works unless mother and father agree. Many new fathers are ambivalent about whether it's okay to sleep with their babies or if they want to sleep with their babies. Dads, if you do have some ambivalence about this sleeping arrangement, my first advice is to trust your wife's intuition concerning what is best for your individual baby. Fathers who have adopted an open attitude have generally come to enjoy sharing sleep.

Let me share with you my personal experience which parallels that of many other fathers. Initially I had reservations about the idea of sleeping with our baby. I gave in to my wife's strong conviction that babies are designed to sleep with their mothers and took a "wait-and-see" attitude. But then I came to enjoy this beautiful closeness. Since I did not have as much time with my children as I wanted to, I think that nighttime closeness was a particular advantage for the baby and me. I feel that this arrangement indeed brought us closer together. One of the most beautiful benefits of sleeping with our baby was awakening in the morning and gazing upon the face of our

## Husband As the Barometer

Totally breastfeeding our son on demand led us to try the family bed. A big plus is not having to get out of a warm bed several times a night to feed the baby. We have fine-tuned our nursing techniques so that now neither I nor the baby fully awakens for feedings.

My husband was to be the barometer in this relationship. Wanting to respect his feelings, we decided that if he thought it was not working out, we'd get a crib. We don't have one yet! All three of us enjoy the closeness, and we rest secure knowing the baby is okay—warm, right next to us, and easy to find in the dark.

A drawback is the (lack of) size of our bed. In anticipation of a larger family, we are making plans for a larger bed.

The baby rarely wakes up crying in the morning. We are usually right there, or in the room, and he is content and happy. A nice way to start each day.

contented child lying only a few feet or a few inches away. I grew accustomed to waking up to the beautiful face of a baby next to me.

As a pediatrician, I have always thought that children should go from waking to sleeping as peacefully as possible, that is, they should be parented to bed and parented awake. As a father, I am even more certain that this continuum of waking, sleeping, and then reawakening should be as smooth as possible. Our babies awakened happily because the first sight they saw was their loving parents. I did not consider their presence in our bed as interference but rather as unity. This is a beautiful level of attachment to be on, not feeling that your infant is coming between you but that you are indeed a father-mother-child unit. This feeling of unity at night certainly does carry over into your functioning during the day. For fathers who truly do have ambivalent feelings toward sleeping with your baby, I advise you not to knock it until you have tried it. You may be surprised that this sleeping arrangement brings out your father's intuition and puts the whole idea of a family unit into a new perspective.

## Alternative Sleeping Arrangements

### *The Sidecar Arrangement*

Parents who choose not to have their baby in their bed but still want to sleep close to baby can use the sidecar arrangement. Remove one side rail from the crib and place the sideless crib adjacent to your bed. Clamp the crib to your bed frame to keep it from shifting. Adjust the crib mattress level to the exact level of your mattress. Be sure there is no crevice between your mattress and baby's. This arrangement works well for those families who want to try the family bed but don't have a king-size bed. It's also a good alternative when the baby is such a squirmer that he needs his own space. You can even buy a special baby bed designed to use as a sidecar next to an adult bed. (For more information, contact Arm's Reach Co-Sleeper, 800-954-9353.)

### *The Extended Bed*

As your baby outgrows the sidecar (or is displaced by a newborn) the extended bed is your next step. There are several ways to do this.

1. *Place a twin bed or roll-away bed adjacent to your bed.*

2. *Place a mattress, sleeping bag, or futon on the floor near your bed. This is especially reassuring to the older child*

*The Arm's Reach Co-Sleeper*

*who may periodically need to re-enter his parents' room because of a nightmare or during a time of stress (sickness, moving, school, etc.).*

3. *The wall-to-wall mattress. This arrangement is unusual in our culture but in many other countries such as Japan, the bedroom is one large sleeping mat or mattress.*

## Sleeping with Siblings

Oftentimes a baby sleeps with the parents for the first one or two years (or longer), then is weaned into a sibling's room, and then gradually moves into his own room. Studies have shown that children under three sleep better sharing a bedroom rather than alone in their own rooms. Parents often report that siblings who sleep together quarrel less.

## Child's Own Room

By the age of three years, most children desire private space for their personal belongings. A child's own room helps foster a sense of order (shelves, compartments for toys, pegs for hanging) and a sense of responsibility for caring for his belongings.

*Siblings sleep better together.*

When children go through the stage of wanting more privacy during pre-adolescence, most want their own rooms. Although separate bedrooms may provide each child space for hobbies, special interests, studying, etc., I do not feel that separate bedrooms are important enough to require a family to overextend themselves financially. Mother and father should not have to work longer hours and further separate themselves from their children in order that the children can be separated from each other.

## The Effect of the Family Bed on Self-Esteem and Discipline

Sleeping with your child definitely has benefits for self-esteem and discipline. Welcoming your child into the family bed or bedroom (not just "allowing" this practice) sends the message "You are a special person. We care about you at night just as we care about you during the day." Nighttime parenting, therefore, carries over into the discipline of a child. One of the hallmarks of a disciplined child is a feeling of rightness. A child who feels right is more likely to act right.

Sleeping with your child adds another dimension to the time you spend in sleep. This sleeping arrangement allows sleep time not to be wasted time. The concept of the family bed allows so many "I care" messages to come through to your child, and you convey these messages without even saying a word.

## References

Institute for Reproductive Health. 1994. *Guidelines: Breastfeeding, Family Planning, and the Lactational Amernorrhea Method—LAM.* Washington, DC: Georgetown University.

Madansky, D. and Edelbrock, C. 1990. Cosleeping in a community sample of 2- and 3-year-old children. *Pediatrics* 86:197-203.

Montagu, A. 1978. *Touching: The Human Significance of the Skin.* New York: Harper.

Thevenin, Tine. 1987. *The Family Bed.* Wayne, NJ: Avery Publishing Group.

# Chapter 4

# How to Get Your Baby to Sleep and Stay Asleep

"If only I could get one full night's sleep."

One of the main principles of the attachment style of parenting is enjoying your child. The fact remains that tired parents and tired children simply do not enjoy each other as much as they could if they were well rested. Sleep problems come in several categories: some children do not go to sleep easily; some children go to sleep easily but do not stay asleep; and some exhausting children neither go to sleep nor stay asleep. All three of these nighttime parenting concerns will be covered in this chapter.

## Attachment Parenting Helps Babies Sleep Better

### Relax Your Baby during the Day

It is impossible to separate daytime from nighttime parenting. The parenting you do by day carries over into your parenting style at night just as a child's waking temperament carries over into his sleep patterns. Infants and children who have difficulty settling at night need daytime gentling. This is especially important for those fussy babies who find it difficult to adjust to life outside the womb and need to be "untensed." Gentling your baby during the day helps him organize his sleep patterns

better at night. As you improve your abilities to gentle your
baby your confidence increases, and this carries over into your
ability to gentle your baby at night. Daytime gentling is
discussed throughout this book, particularly in the first chapter.
It includes frequent breastfeeding, "wearing" your baby,
responding to the baby's cries, sleeping with baby, lots of skin-
to-skin contact, and a high level of father involvement.

### Arrive at a Sleeping Arrangement that Works

Start off with your baby in your bed right away before the usual
nighttime crying begins or take your baby into your bed as
soon as he begins to give you cues that he does not want to
sleep alone. Most sleep problems can either be prevented or
alleviated by sleeping with your baby. This allows harmony to
develop between you and your infant in the first few months,
and it prepares you for the nighttime parenting which lies
ahead. Bringing your baby into your bed as a last resort usually
does not work as well. Solving problems rather than preventing
them from happening ("catch-up parenting") is a strain on both
parents and child. Try to stay one step ahead of your child. You
are creating habits, good habits.

Children often give very clear cues that they want and need
to sleep close to their parents. For example, parents will wake
up in the morning and find their two-year-old sound asleep on
the floor just outside their closed bedroom door. If the concept
of the family bed is not attractive to you, then consider
alternative sleeping arrangements: a crib adjacent to your bed,
a mattress or sleeping bag on the floor next to your bed, or
siblings sleeping together.

### How to Condition Your Baby or Child for Sleep

While I do not believe in rigid schedules and regimented
nighttime parenting, it is true that to a certain extent sleep
habits in babies are a learned response and a certain amount of
conditioning may be necessary to help some babies fall off to
sleep. It is important that when babies are presented with
certain cues they know that sleep is expected of them. Bedtime
rituals set the stage and convey the message that sleep is soon
to follow. Children should learn that a bed is for sleeping or for
quiet communication, not for wrestling or playing.

## Bedtime

Ordinarily schedule is a bad word in the general style of attachment parenting. However, when it comes to inducing sleep, some children do seem to need predictable bedtimes and nap times. If this works for your family then try the set bedtime routine. Many children, especially high need children, are very resistant to any regimenting of either their daytime or their nighttime sleep-wake patterns. Bedtime does not have to mean sleep time. Sleep is not a state you can force children into. Sleep must overtake the child. Parents' role is to create a sleep-inducing environment. Older children (ages three or four and up) and certainly school-age children need a consistent bedtime when they should settle down in their beds.

Some parents have rigid and unrealistic definitions of bedtime: "Thou shalt go to bed at seven o'clock." At the other extreme, some parents define bedtime as whenever the child falls asleep. Because of changing lifestyles and family situations, rigid bedtimes are not as common or as realistic as they used to be. The textbook baby who sleeps from 7:00 P.M. to 8:00 A.M. may miss a lot of prime-time parenting, especially from father. (Actually, this baby exists only in textbooks.)

There seem to be two reasons why parents are eager for early bedtimes: mother is worn out by the end of the day, and father does not enjoy spending an evening with a cranky and tired child. These concerns do have a remedy. Create conditions in your home which make it possible to enjoy the baby or child in the evening. Encourage a late afternoon nap so that when dad arrives home, father and child can enjoy this prime time together, and mother can get some much-needed relief. Don't feel that you are breaking unwritten rules if your baby's bedtime is not until nine or ten o'clock or even as late as when you go to bed. This unconventional bedtime may occur particularly in large and busy families or in families where the father does not get home from work until late. Babies will often arrive at a sleep-wake schedule that best fits their needs within the family situation.

This was true in our own family when our daughter Erin was a baby. In the morning, the household was very busy as her four older siblings got up and going. Erin learned to sleep through this chaos and awakened around 9:30 A.M. The older children returned home from school around 3:30 P.M., so Erin learned to take her nap from 3:30 to 5:30. The chaos settled down around mealtime when Daddy came home. By then Erin was awake and refreshed and ready to enjoy a full evening of prime time with her family. She then willingly fell asleep around ten o'clock; sometimes she was awake until her mother and I went to bed. For most children, the ritual of going to bed is more important than when they go to bed.

I freely admit that all parents occasionally feel that they are ready for the child to go to bed so they can have some quiet time together. But one of the red flags that signals early disharmony in the family is a mother telling me that dad is really pressuring her to get the child off to bed early. This usually means that there is some fundamental breakdown in the understanding of nighttime parenting and enjoyment of the child.

In our own family, Martha and I have always enjoyed having "dinner for two" at home once a week. The older children minister to the younger children, and mom and dad enjoy some quiet time. The older children have learned to respect this special time that mom and dad have together, but at times when there was a nursing baby in the house, this quiet evening often turned out to be dinner for three.

### Create Parenting-to-Sleep Routines

Very seldom can infants be expected to fall asleep by themselves. They cannot go from a state of being awake directly into deep sleep. They must go through a period of REM or active sleep first. Routines for parenting to sleep are designed to get the baby through the REM stage. If you try to put your baby down into bed before he has completed the REM stage of sleep (which averages around twenty minutes) and before he has entered deep sleep, he is likely to awaken as soon as you try to sneak out of the room.

It will save you a lot of energy if you wait until your baby is fully asleep in your arms or at your breast before you put him down. I call this "nursing down."

You can develop bedtime rituals that will induce sleep in your baby. Nursing and a rocking chair are usually a winning combination for inducing sleep. Plan to be your newborn's moving bed. One of the tell-tale signs that a woman is a mother of a new baby is that she is always swaying back and forth a bit. She is simulating the motion the baby has been accustomed to during nine months in the womb. Other "back to the womb" activities are also helpful in the art of nighttime parenting.

**Baths.** A warm bath before bedtime and a soothing massage will often relax both of you. You can take the baby in the tub with you. The soothing skin-to-skin contact will prepare baby to accept the rest of the parenting-to-sleep ritual.

**Swaddling.** Babies differ in how they like to be wrapped at bedtime. Some babies settle better in loose coverings which allow them more freedom of movement; others prefer to be securely swaddled in cotton sheets or baby blankets. Some babies like to "sleep tight," others like to "sleep loose." A mother once shared with me that she dressed her baby loosely during the day and swaddled him at night. This helped condition her baby to associate sleep with swaddling.

**Lie down with your baby.** Your baby may be ready to fall asleep, but he just doesn't want to be put down alone. Rock and nurse him to sleep in your arms, either while walking or in a rocking chair. Then lie down with your sleeping baby on your bed and extend this time together a bit longer until you are certain your baby is sound asleep (or until you are sound asleep). My wife calls this ritual nestle nursing. You'll know your baby is asleep when the sucking stops, the jaw loosens, and baby lets go of the nipple or you can ease it out of his mouth. The breast is still the oldest, most effective, safest, and certainly most beautifully packaged sleeping pill. This smooth continuum from a warm bath to warm arms to warm breast to a warm bed will usually induce sleep in one (or both) of you.

**Cradles and other moving beds.** After you have parented your baby to sleep on your own bed, you can either leave him there or move him into his own bed. Some babies will allow themselves to be parented to sleep in arms and then placed down in the cradle or crib. If your baby is sensitive to cold bed sheets, warm the sheet or crib pad in the dryer or with a heating pad.

As soon as you put your baby down in the cradle continue a gentle rocking until he seems to have completely settled into the stage of deep sleep. Rocking in general, whether in your arms or in a cradle, should be around sixty beats per minute, the heartbeat rhythm that your baby has grown accustomed to *in utero*. If you don't have a cradle, putting little roller wheels on baby's bed and gently rolling it back and forth a few inches may lull baby to sleep. This technique is often used in hospitals where all baby beds have rollers.

**Laying on of hands.** Immediately after being put down to bed, some babies will squirm a bit and their heads will bob up and down, giving you the signal that they are not in deep enough sleep to be left alone. In this case, father (he has a bigger hand) can lay his hand on the back or the head of the baby, or put one hand on the head and one on the back. The warmth of a secure hand may be the added touch that is needed to help baby give up his silent protest and drift off to sleep. Patting baby's back or bottom rhythmically at sixty beats per minute may add the finishing touches to the ritual of inducing sleep. Remove your hands gradually, first one, then the other, easing the pressure slowly so as not to startle the baby back to waking. His sense of your touch is very keen. We have observed an interesting phenomenon in our babies: you must be very gradual in removing your hand, even allowing it to hover just above your baby's skin before removing it completely.

**Baby's sleeping position.** Lay your baby down to sleep on his back. Studies have shown that babies who sleep on their backs are at a lower risk for SIDS, and recent "back to sleep" public information campaigns have brought about significant reductions in SIDS rates in many countries around the world. No one knows why the back sleeping position is associated with lower SIDS rates. For some possible explanations, see Chapter Twelve.

There are some medical situations in which a doctor may advise that a baby sleep on his stomach. These include prematurity and gastroesophageal reflux. Check with your doctor if you think your baby would be better off sleeping on his stomach.

Some babies do not like being put down on their backs when they are tired. This is another reason for parenting your baby to sleep in your arms. Once your baby is in a deep sleep, he won't resist being put down on his back. The side-sleeping position is also associated with a lower risk of SIDS, though SIDS authorities are concerned that a baby put down to sleep on his side may well roll onto his stomach. If your baby prefers to sleep on his side, gently extend his bottom arm forward in front of him, at a ninety-degree angle to his body. This makes it more difficult for him to roll onto his tummy.

The association between tummy-sleeping and increased SIDS is only a statistical one, true for large study populations. Your baby, however, is an individual. If, after you've encouraged him to sleep on his back, your baby clearly prefers to sleep on his stomach, let him, and don't worry about it. Many other factors are involved in SIDS risk, including parental smoking and lack of breastfeeding. Sleeping position is only one part of the SIDS story. Also, the risk of SIDS decreases significantly after six months of age; once your baby has passed this milestone, you no longer need to be concerned about his sleeping position.

**Help your baby snuggle.** Instead of placing baby in the center of the crib or cradle, place him in touch with one side. Babies seem to like the security of sleeping against an object or person. This explains why babies often squirm their way into the corner of the crib, against the side rail, or against mommy or daddy in the family bed.

**Sounds of the womb.** Sounds help to induce sleep and especially to keep a baby sleeping. Babies often settle best with what is known as "white noise," sounds involving all the frequencies audible to the human ear such as the fan of an air conditioner, a dishwasher, or a vacuum cleaner. This noise is repetitive and without meaning and lulls the mind into oblivion. The most effective sleep-inducing sounds are those which most closely resemble the rhythm and sounds of the womb: running water from a nearby faucet or shower, a metronome set at sixty beats per minute, a ticking clock, a recording of womb sounds, a bubbling fish tank, or waterfall or ocean sounds. Tape record the sounds for sleep that work best for your baby. Use a tape player with automatic replay that keeps on playing. Babies settle better with classical music rather than turbulent rock music. Choose music which is simple and consistent, such as flute and classical guitar. Studies have shown that even unborn babies were calmed by the music of Mozart and Vivaldi but were excited by rock (Verny 1981). Select a medley of pieces which soothe your baby and prepare a continuous tape from recordings of these pieces.

One of the parents in my practice, Robert Evenden, a professor of music, selected the following program to calm and induce sleep in his high need baby and tired wife:

> *Antonin Dvorak, Serenade for Strings, opus 22, second movement*
>
> *Claude Debussy, "Prelude on the Afternoon of a Faun"*
>
> *Claude Debussy, "Clair de Lune"*
>
> *Maurice Ravel, "Pavane for a Dead Princess"*
>
> *W. A. Mozart, Symphony No. 17 in G Major, K. 129, first movement*

Other selected soothing works:

> *J. S. Bach, Third Brandenburg Concerto*
>
> *J. S. Bach,* The Well-Tempered Clavier, *Parts I and II*
>
> *Franz Joseph Haydn, string quartets.*
>
> *Maurice Ravel, piano works.*
>
> *W. A. Mozart, string divertimenti, early symphonies*
>
> *Claude Debussy, "Dances Sacred and Profane," piano preludes*

**A warm fuzzy.** Dad's chest is a "warm fuzzy" place that often induces sleep in the tiny baby who is small enough not to wriggle off easily. Another "warm fuzzy" is a lambskin. In Australia and New Zealand, parents report that babies seem to sleep better when placed on a lambskin mat. These mats are specially shorn to be both safe and comfortable for babies as

*A "warm fuzzy."*

well as machine washable. If your baby gets a stuffy nose from
the lint, cover the lambskin with a sheet or cloth diaper. Be
sure your baby is not allergic to wool (no persistent sniffles or
skin rashes). Lambskin mats also help in the conditioning of
babies to sleep. Many mothers will take the lambskin with them
wherever they go so that when baby is placed on the lambskin
"bed," he is encouraged to nap. When I gave parenting talks in
Australia, it was beautiful to look out into the audience and see
babies napping and feeling right at home on their lambskin
mats, placed at their parents' feet.

**A bed on wheels.** Sometimes your baby may be particularly
fussy. You know he is ready for sleep, and certainly you're
ready for him to be ready for sleep. Nevertheless, no sleep-
inducing tips or tricks are working. Try this as a last resort: put
your baby in a safe car seat and go for a ride. Non-stop motion
is the best. I call this "freeway fathering." When your baby has
fallen into a deep sleep, return home and place your sleeping
baby into his room or your bedroom. Don't try to remove him
from the car seat or he will probably awaken. Going for a drive
with the baby is especially helpful when mom and dad need a
time and place for some uninterrupted communication.

## Parenting a Baby Back to Sleep

**Create a quiet environment for sleep.** Parents are concerned not only with getting their baby to sleep but also with keeping their baby asleep. For most sleeping babies you don't have to tiptoe around and create a noiseless environment. The more common arousal stimuli are startling noises, light, hunger, loneliness, and discomfort. You can create a calmer sleeping environment by lessening these stimuli.

1. *Provide a warm body to sleep with.*
2. *Soundproof the sleeping area as much as possible. Oil the springs and joints of a squeaky crib. Put the barking dog in the garage at night—before it barks. Take the phone off the hook.*
3. *If your child has a pain-producing illness or discomfort such as teething, check with your doctor about giving the appropriate dosage of pain-relieving medication.*
4. *Use opaque shades to block out light.*

**Respond quickly to your baby's awakening signal.** The most vulnerable period for awakening is when a baby ascends from deep sleep into light sleep. Sometimes babies will whimper and squirm for a few seconds and resettle themselves without any outside help as they pass through this vulnerable period. When baby awakens during this vulnerable period get to him quickly. Soothe him with nursing or a reassuring laying-on of hands. If you parent your baby through this vulnerable period, you can prevent him from awakening completely.

I have noticed that during this vulnerable period my own babies seem to direct their radar systems toward mommy and move in to nurse. The more easily available their target, the less they awaken.

**Middle of the night conditioning.** Some infants and children awaken in the middle of the night ready to play. Here is where conditioning is often necessary for sheer parental survival. When all the above sleep-inducing tips don't work to get a child back to sleep, simply let the baby sit there next to you in bed while you continue sleeping (or pretending to sleep), ignoring her desire to play. Again you are conveying the non-negotiable

# Playtime at Four in the Morning

*"Our one-and-a-half-year-old baby awakens around 3:00 or 4:00 A.M., happy, and wide awake and ready to play. I'm not ready to play at that hour."*

Prior to fifteen months a child does not usually understand any form of verbal negotiation about when it is playtime and when it isn't. However, between eighteen months and two years children have enough receptive language to understand an admonition that nighttime is for sleeping. Adopting a later bedtime and/or shorter daytime naps may discourage middle-of-the-night waking. Children who are put down for bed around 7:00 P.M. frequently do awaken about 4:00 A.M., ready to go. Obviously, this baby is slept out; nine hours of nighttime sleep plus one hour of nap time gives him a total of ten hours, which for some babies is enough sleep. In general, babies who do awaken frequently to play need a bit of conditioning; the bed and the bedroom are for sleeping and not for playing.

---

message to your child that if he is in bed with you, he sleeps when you sleep and does not play.

**A full tummy, but not too full.** A stomach that is too full or too empty will interfere with sleep. Nursing the baby before bedtime usually suffices to fill up the tummy of the young infant. Stuffing your baby full of cereal to get him to sleep through the night usually doesn't work. A glass of milk and a nutritious cookie, a bowl of cereal, or some fruit are all good bedtime snacks for the young child.

**Nighttime changing tips.** Double-diapering your baby may lessen the sensation of wetness. Change him before night feedings rather than after (although you may have to change diapers again). If baby is sleeping in your bed, keep an extra supply of diapers and baby wipes within easy reaching distance. A night light or the room light on a low dimmer makes it easier to identify baby's diapering needs. A flannel-backed rubber pad under baby will protect your mattress from nighttime accidents.

**Leave a little bit of mother behind.** If you have a baby who is very sensitive to separation and you must be away from him when he is sleeping, he may settle better if you leave behind an object that he associates with you. One mother of a tiny baby noticed that her baby settled better when she left her nursing bra in the cradle. A tape recording of you singing a bedtime song or lullaby may help.

Mother substitutes have become big business. A newspaper story reported that researchers at the University of California developed a teddy bear which has a breathing mechanism that can be synchronized with the baby's own breathing. Baby can snuggle up to the breathing bear. One mother, in a letter to the editor, wrote, "Why not use the real mother?"

**Enticing the early riser to sleep in.** The child who pops into your bedroom at 5:00 A.M. and wants to play can be a trial to tired parents. Purists may claim that a baby should be allowed to follow his own biorhythms for awakening at dawn. It's easy to say this about someone else's baby. Babies can be fooled as to what time it really is. Oftentimes a slight bit of light coming through the windows at dawn is just enough to awaken a baby, especially if that ray of light happens to strike during a period in a child's sleep cycle when he is vulnerable to being awakened. The following suggestions may prolong sleep in your early riser:

*Lay down rules for noiseless waking with the early riser's older siblings.*
*Dark, opaque curtains may prolong the nighttime environment.*
*Give the child an alarm clock "just like Daddy's." When the alarm goes off, the child may get up, just like Daddy does. Leave a box of things to do beside your child's bed in order to entice him to stay in his room and play quietly by himself for a while.*
*Leave a nutritious snack on a bedside table to tide the hungry riser over until breakfast*

## *Bedtime Rituals for Older Infants and Children*

There are nights when you know your child is tired, but he just won't give up and go to bed. The problem is not that your child doesn't want to go to bed; it's that he doesn't want to be separated from you. What he has to give up causes the protest. Creative bedtime rituals and intuitive nighttime parenting can overcome both of these reasons for not wanting to go to sleep. Older infants and children often need "wind-down" activities such as a warm bath, a soothing story, a back rub, gradually dimming lights (a dimmer switch in a child's bedroom is a wise investment), and bedtime prayers. Lying down with your child and mothering or fathering him to sleep can often alleviate the separation sensitivity that is really the main reason why children don't want to give up and fall asleep. Avoid exciting and stimulating activities such as wrestling immediately before bedtime. These may only serve to fire up the engine that is already unwilling to wind down. There are special circumstances in which a child may demand a very long and exhausting bedtime ritual because he needs it. These are discussed in the chapter on nighttime fathering.

The following bedtime tips were given to me by creative parents of older children:

> *An alarm clock buzzer to signal "bedtime in five minutes."*
> *To avoid a conflict of wills, let the clock announce bedtime.*
> *A game of "whoever is in bed first picks the story."*
> *Massage game. "Keep your eyes closed. Don't peek. What am I rubbing now?"*
> *Back-rub game. "Plant" a garden on your child's back, using different touches for different foods which your child selects. Gradually lighten your strokes as you smooth out the garden.*
> *Use an egg timer. "When all the sand hits the bottom, the lights must go out." Your child may get tired watching the sand fall.*

**Bedtime stories.** The baby in the womb knows his mother's voice (and father's, too, if care is taken to project it closely against the mother's abdomen). Studies have shown that the

unborn baby responds to the mother's voice physically with synchronized body movements (Verny 1981). Right after birth it is important for the baby to hear this familiar voice talking, singing, and humming so that he will know and trust that he is as secure as he felt before birth. A study at the University of North Carolina showed that infants remembered what their mothers read to them while in the womb. Babies in this study responded more strongly after birth to stories they had heard while in the womb than to others by the same author.

Of course your voice can be given to your baby spontaneously without books most of the time, but at certain times of the day you can recite or read a favorite lullaby or ditty, nursery rhyme, or poem. As you have the time, inclination, and resources, start to collect books that strike your fancy and that you know will appeal to your baby. Look for sounds that are repetitive, rhyming, flowing, lulling, and comforting. Choose a book that you enjoy, too, so when your little one says "Read it again," you won't mind complying. Books can supply the creative bent you may feel you lack, especially on those days when fatigue saps all of your poetic flair. The baby will respond to the warmth in your voice and to the enthusiasm and love he hears. He will feel wrapped in your voice as surely as he feels wrapped in your arms. This will be the beginning of a long happy tradition of reading at those special times of day when you want to help your baby or child relax.

Bedtime will be the most honored time of all for stories, and your child will not outgrow being read to until well into his school years. Our teenagers still come to listen occasionally to the stories we read to our younger children. A bedtime story, followed perhaps by a tender bedtime prayer, is a wonderful way to launch your nighttime parenting. Here are a few tried-

and-true family favorites:

Bedtime for Frances *by Russell Hoban. Harper, 1976.*
(*Ages two to five years.*)
A Bedtime Story *by Joan Levine. Dutton, 1975.*
(*Four to six years.*)
Blueberries for Sal *by Robert McCloskey. Puffin, 1976.*
(*One to four years.*)
Goodnight Moon *by Margaret Wise Brown. Harper, 1947.*
(*One to three years.*)
Harry the Dirty Dog *by Gene Zion. Harper, 1976.*
(*Two to six years.*)
A Hole is to Dig *by Ruth Krauss. Harper, 1952.*
(*Two to five years.*)
Max's First Word *by Rosemary Wells. Dial, 1979.*
(*One to two years.*)
Noah's Ark *by Peter Spier. Doubleday, 1977.*
(*One to four years.*)
Our Best Friends *by Gyo Fujikawa. Zokeisha, 1977.*
(*Two to four years.*)
Pat the Bunny *by Dorothy Kunhardt. Golden, 1962.*
(*One to two years.*)
The Little Engine That Could *by Watty Piper. Platt, 1961.*
(*Two to four years.*)
The Poky Little Puppy *by Janette S. Lowrey. Golden, 1942.*
(*Two to four years.*)
The Three Little Pigs *by Paul Galdone. Seabury, 1970.*
(*Two to four years.*)
Tikki Tikki Tembo *by Arlene Mosel. Holt, 1968.*
(*Three to four years.*)
Where's Spot? *by Eric Hill. Putnam, 1980.*
(*Two to five years.*)

**Modeling.** The concept of modeling applies to parenting-to-sleep routines. One day our six-year-old daughter, Hayden, and her friends played "putting Erin to sleep." Hayden lay down next to Erin, pulled her in close, and pretended to nurse her while everyone sang lullabies. These children had learned the important lesson that babies do not go off to sleep alone.

# What about Sleeping Medications?

In general, both parents and doctors are reluctant to give sleeping medications to babies. I share this reluctance and do not prescribe sleep medications for babies under nine months. There are, however, situations which may warrant the use of sleeping medications. When used with the direction of a physician, sleep medications are safe and effective for inducing sleep in your baby. If, in a difficult situation, you've tried all the natural methods of nighttime parenting, but the family is nevertheless falling apart from stress and fatigue, so that daytime parenting as well as nighttime parenting is severely compromised–in this extreme case, when child abuse seems imminent, one to three nights' use of a sleeping medication seems appropriate. One should exercise great caution in using sleeping medications for more than a few nights, since infants build up a tolerance rather quickly and can easily become addicted. Sleeping medications can also be "habit-forming" for the mother: they discourage her from relying on her intuitive nighttime mothering. Also, most sleeping medications do not induce normal sleep, but often interfere with the usual sleep stages and may impair functioning the following day.

In my medical experience, the prescription drug chloral hydrate (Noctec) is the most safe and effective sleep-inducing medication for infants and children. Chloral hydrate has also been found not to have an abnormal effect on sleep stages (Kales 1970). Other medications which are often prescribed to induce sleep, such as antihistamines and barbiturates, may have the opposite effect in infants and children, that is, they wind them up, instead of winding them down. In my experience and in studies in the medical literature, sleeping medications such as chloral hydrate only work about half the time and at best have only a temporary effect on an infant's sleep patterns (Chavin 1980).

# A Happy Beginning, a Loving Ending

The last words you speak to your child at night and the first words you say to him in the morning should be warm and personal and should leave an inner feeling of rightness with the child. A practice which we have enjoyed in our family is to convey a very personal "love thought" when our children go to bed and when they get up. Each night before going to sleep my children have heard from me how much I love them and how much I really care for them. I have tried to tell them in a different way each night, and our children have looked forward to hearing a simple but sincere and different "love thought" from night to night. Parents can influence their child's dreams for the better by providing a bedtime ritual in which the last faces the child sees before drifting off to sleep are those of his parents and the last words he hears are "I love you."

**References**

Chavin, W. 1980. Children with sleep difficulties. *Health Visitor* 53:447.

Kales, A. C. 1970. Hypnotic drugs and their effectiveness. *Arch Gen Psychiatr* 23:226.

Mitchell, E. A. 1991. Sleeping position and cot deaths. *Lancet* 338:192.

Verny, T. 1981. *The Secret Life of the Unborn Child.* New York: Dell.

# Chapter 5
## Should Baby Cry It Out?

"Doctor, is it all right to let my baby cry it out when he awakens in the middle of the night?"

To gather information for this book I sent questionnaires to several hundred parents. One of the questions was, "What advice do you get from friends and relatives about what to do when your baby awakens during the night?" The most common advice offered was, "Let the baby cry it out." In this questionnaire I also asked parents to tell me how they felt about this advice. Ninety-five percent of the mothers responded that this advice did not feel right. I concluded that 95 percent of mothers can't be wrong and that there is often a real conflict between what a  mother hears from advisors and what she feels. Because of the widespread confusion about this "to cry or not to cry it out" question, I have written this chapter to help parents arrive at answers which are best for their individual family situations.

I have learned during my years as a pediatrician that difficult problems in child-rearing do not have easy answers. How you respond to your baby's cries is certainly one of those perplexing questions in which an easy answer would be presumptuous on the part of the advisor and unfair to both the listening parent and the crying infant. This is not a "let your baby cry" book. Instead, NIGHTTIME PARENTING is a book

designed to help individual parents become confident and
comfortable in responding to their own babies' cries.

## How the Mother-Baby Communication Network Develops

A mother once said to me,
"If only she could talk, I would
know what my baby needs when
she awakens." I sympathized
with her but responded, "Your
baby can talk. You just need to
learn how to listen."

The cry of an infant is more
than just a sound. It is a signal
intended to influence the
behavior of another. The signal of the infant's cry releases the
mother's emotions. It does something to the mother, and that's
what makes the mother-baby crying communication network so
special. In response to her own baby's cry, the mother's body
chemistry changes. When a mother hears or sees her own baby
cry, she experiences a surge of hormones within her body and
an increase in blood flow to her breasts that trigger the urge to
pick up the baby and nurse.

There are two parts to this communication network: the
transmitter (the baby) and the receiver (the parent). The value
of the cry depends upon the infant properly emitting it and the
listener correctly perceiving it. When the baby's nighttime cries
are properly attended to, he learns to trust that his actions can
affect others. The infant learns that he has value. This is the
beginning of self-esteem. A mother who follows her instinctual
urge to respond promptly to her crying baby develops her own
sensitivity. The more she responds to her baby's cries the more
sensitive she becomes to the meaning of her baby's language.
The combination of baby's trust and mother's sensitivity gets
nighttime parenting off to the right start.

## *How Letting the Baby Cry Affects the Mother*

Admonitions to let the baby cry it out confuse the new mother. The infant's cry releases a mother's caretaking emotions, an indication that a mother is not designed to let her own baby cry, nor is the baby designed to be left alone crying. When this design is not followed, disharmony results, and a little red flag inside the mother waves, "Something is not quite right here."

A baby has a need. A mother responds to that need. This is a special mother-baby communication network uniquely designed for the survival of the baby and the development of the mother. Any advice that runs counter to this communication network sets off an internal alarm within the mother which says, "Not right." This inner feeling about letting her baby cry is a fail-safe mechanism that ensures that the baby gets mothered. These are healthy internal signals. Listen to them, they will never fail you.

A confused mother told me about one night when she followed the "let the baby cry" advice because it came from her own mother. I asked. "Did it work?" She responded, "Not only did it not work, but I felt so guilty." I smiled. "Good, that means you are becoming a sensitive mother."

Letting the baby cry undermines a mother's confidence and intuition. As I discussed above, not responding to a baby's cries goes against most mothers' intuitive responses. If a mother consistently goes against what she feels, she begins to desensitize herself to the signal value of her baby's cries. The less intuitively a mother responds, the less confidence she has in the appropriateness of her responses. The less confidence she has, the less likely that her responses are appropriate, and the less she enjoys mothering. A mother who restrains herself from responding to her baby gradually and unknowingly becomes insensitive. This is the vicious cycle of detachment which I urge new mothers not to let themselves get into. Once you allow outside advice to overtake your own intuitive mothering you and your child are at risk of drifting apart.

Some new mothers will confide in me, "But I don't feel like I have any intuition. I really am confused. Sometimes I don't know whether or not to rush in and pick up my crying baby at three in the morning."

## Never Again

*Well-meaning friends and relatives said "Let the baby cry. After a half-hour, he'll be asleep and he'll never wake up at night again." We tried it once but couldn't get beyond the first ten minutes, both of us rushing in to comfort a sobbing, shaking and very scared baby. We never tried that again.*

Building up a sensitivity to your baby's cues is one way your intuition matures. Promptly responding to your baby's cries helps develop your sensitivity. Restraining yourself from responding makes you insensitive, and insensitivity gets a new mother into trouble. Guilt is a healthy reaction when some inner set of rules, some inner instinct has not been followed. This is exactly what happened in the mother who described herself as feeling guilty. She allowed herself to do something which went against her inner mothering rules, and naturally she did not feel right about it. Most of a mother's guilt feelings are caused by outside advice which runs contrary to her own intuition. The advisors are the ones who should be bothered by guilt, not the mother.

The attachment style of parenting, especially where it involves promptly responding to a baby's crying, is tailor-made for those mothers who are a bit shaky about their own intuition. Your crying baby will help you develop your responding instinct if you allow yourself to listen to your baby. On the other hand, parenting with restrained responses hinders the development of your mothering intuition.

### How Letting the Baby Cry Affects Him

A restrained response to crying undermines the infant's trust. Throughout this book, I have repeatedly mentioned that trust between parent and child is indispensable to child-rearing. Researchers in children's personality development mention trust as one of the prime determinants of a child's personality. If a child is trusted, he learns how to trust. Trust your infant: trust that he is crying because he has a need. Trust yourself when you perceive crying as a stimulus which demands a response. The more you trust your infant's signals, the more your infant trusts himself. Remember, that it is a person who is crying. Give the unborn child, the newborn, the infant, and the child the status of personhood. They feel and cry just like an older person. Respond to your baby. Trust begins by instilling in baby the feeling that distress will be followed by comfort.

## Does Letting the Baby Cry Work?

When I interview parents who have allowed themselves to be talked into letting their baby cry it out in the middle of the night, they tell me it doesn't work. An occasional parent will report that the baby, when left to cry, did stop, but the effects were less than desirable.

Lori, an exhausted mother of a night-waking baby, in desperation succumbed to the restrained response advice. "I plugged my ears and let him cry," she said. "My husband had to hold me down as I deeply wanted to go pick him up. The baby's cries got louder and louder, and finally I couldn't stand it any longer and went in to him. Boy, was he mad! I'll never do that again."

Another failure of the restrained response approach was shared with me by a mother whose doctor advised her to let her night-waking baby cry it out. "I couldn't stand it any longer, and I finally went in to nurse him back to sleep. We both sat there in the rocking chair crying together, and it took me twice as long to nurse him back to sleep than if I had gone to him immediately. The next day he was clinging to me all day long."

This mother learned an important fact of midnight mothering: the quicker a cry is responded to, the easier it is to turn it off. The baby's clinginess the next day was an emotional response to his trust having been temporarily shattered.

When you use the non-responding approach, you are using the principle of non-reinforcement: if you do not reinforce a behavior, the behavior soon stops. This behavioristic approach bothers me for two reasons. First, it assumes that the baby's crying is a negative behavior which should be extinguished, a false assumption. Secondly, it may have a damaging effect on the baby's emerging self-esteem. When a baby cries and no one listens, the baby's internal motivation for crying lessens. One of the fundamental principles of infant growth and development is that an appropriate response to a skill or an action is one of the prime motivating factors for continued development of that skill. If the baby's cries fall on dead ears, he is less motivated to cry. (This is why non-reinforcement seems to work.) However, a baby's cries are a baby's language. Primitive though it may be, crying is a tiny baby's only network of communication to the outside world. Taking away this form of communication may have a carry-over effect on the general desire to communicate to caregivers. Mothers will sometimes report that after a night of letting the baby cry, he gives them the cold shoulder the next day. As the baby loses trust in his ability to communicate, he also loses trust that the caregiver will respond. The "let cry" advice may produce a short-term gain, but a long-term loss. In my opinion, opting for the short-term gain is not a wise choice.

Another defense of the unresponsive approach is that the baby must learn to sleep. But you are not really teaching the baby to sleep by not responding to his cries; you are teaching your baby that cries have no communicative value. When cries are not responded to, a baby may fall back to sleep on his own, but this is a sign of withdrawal following the disappointment of not being listened to. By not giving in to your baby you are teaching him to give up. I have great difficulty with the wisdom of this approach. It is night training, not nighttime parenting. We train pets, we parent children. Parents, you need not worry that by promptly responding to your baby's cries you are reinforcing crying behavior and creating a whining, crying child. Studies have shown that young babies whose cries are promptly responded to cry less as older infants (Bell and Ainsworth 1972). Responding to your baby does not produce "trained night crying," as some experts warn. Instead it will eventually teach your child to cry less.

"But you're creating a habit" is another way to justify the restrained approach. There is often a very fine line between a habit and a need. A habit is usually considered to be a pattern of behavior acquired by frequent repetition that a person can get rid of with no resulting harm. A need, on the other hand, is necessary for the proper functioning of the individual. A habit, if not responded to, will easily go away. A need does not go away so easily. An unfulfilled need is never completely erased; it is only temporarily suppressed and will flare up again in a different way. In general, if you recognize that your child's desire for nighttime parenting is a need to be filled and not a habit to be broken, you both will eventually receive the pay-off of fewer sleepless nights once the child's need is fulfilled.

Distinguishing between habit and need is often wasted mental energy. I usually assume the behaviors of young infants are needs which, if appropriately filled, may certainly become habits because the infant likes the way he feels when a need is filled. In short, babies have habitual needs, but the habit they get into is the habit of feeling right. The continual feeling of rightness has a positive effect on self-esteem and personality. The habit of feeling "not right" may contribute to an angry, difficult baby who is not a joy to parent.

The temperament of the baby also influences whether or not the "let your baby cry" advice should be used. High need babies rarely respond to the restrained approach. They learn to cry harder, longer, and with more disturbing cries. These babies send the unmistakable message that they need a high level of nighttime parenting. These babies are also endowed with a temperament that stimulates them to protest vehemently if their needs are not met. The habit (or need) of night-waking should not be broken in high need babies.

Babies with easier temperaments usually do not exhibit night-waking cries that activate the red-alert response in the mother. Easy babies seem more capable of self-soothing and may not elicit as prompt a response to their night-waking cries. Be especially vigilant about the so-called easy baby. These babies are a mixed blessing. They are endowed with self-soothing abilities which take some pressure off the mother. However, they also lack certain attachment-promoting behaviors (for example, protest cries when a need is not being filled) which are important to the development of their personalities and their mothers' skills.

Experienced mothers can often tell a "red alert" cry from a "hold off a bit" cry by the demanding nature of the cry and how

━━━━━━━━━━ *Short-Circuiting Nighttime Crying* ━━━━━━━━━━

> One of the best things about bringing the baby to bed
> with us is that it usually only takes a little patting on the
> back to put her to sleep again. Otherwise, if she's in her
> crib, by the time I get out of bed and into her room, she's
> worked herself into a more wakeful cry and it's much
> harder to put her back to sleep. By the time I'm done
> settling her, I'm wide awake, and it's harder for me to go
> back to sleep. But when she's in bed with us, I catch her
> on the first little peep and I don't have to get out of bed.

quickly it diminishes. The cries of high need babies usually
build up momentum until anyone in earshot must respond. The
cries of the easy baby may diminish more quickly, and the baby
may resettle without outside intervention. Whether or not to
respond to a baby's night-waking cries is a judgment call. Only
the mother has the sensitivity to make this judgment.

## The Ultimate in Nighttime Sensitivity

The ultimate in nighttime harmony is a sleeping arrangement
in which the baby does not have to cry to get his needs met.
When mothers and babies sleep close to each other, their sleep
cycles are synchronized. The mother becomes sensitive to the
signals of her awakening baby and intervenes quickly before
crying is necessary. Chapter Three discusses the concept of
sharing sleep and how it helps mother and baby achieve
nighttime harmony.

I advise parents to respond promptly to their baby's night-
waking cries. Don't let yourself fall prey to the restrained
response approach. Start off being open to your new baby's
cries. As you and the baby develop your communication
network, your baby will learn to cry better, you will learn to
listen better, and all of you will sleep better, knowing that you
have learned to respond to each other.

### References

Bell, S. M. and Ainsworth, M. D. 1972. Infant crying and maternal
responsiveness. *Child Development* 43:1171.

# Chapter 6

# Food for Sleep

The food your child eats and how it is "served" can have a profound effect on his sleep. Babies have a vulnerable period for awakening when they go from quiet to active sleep. This vulnerable period is when most infants who share sleep with their mothers will start sucking. The brain needs to eat when it becomes active. Breastfeeding (both the act of breastfeeding and the content of the breast milk) is an ideal "food" for sleep.

## Breastfeeding Helps Nighttime Parenting

### *A Harmonious Relationship*
Breastfeeding has a beneficial effect on the sleep-wake rhythm in experimental animals. Researchers found that the harmony between a mother and her suckling infant had an organizing effect on the baby's sleep pattern (Hofer and Shair 1982). In another study, the authors comment, "The mother apparently exerts a regulatory effect on the organization of the infant's sleep-wake cycle through the periodicity of her delivery of nutrient" (Hofer 1982).

### *Sharing Sleep*
There are only a few studies of the effects of breastfeeding on sleep and dream cycles. Researchers have found that breastfeeding infants show REM sleep patterns when sucking

during sleep. This is often called sucking REM. The breastfeeding mother and infant dream in unison, and mothers experience one of the highest levels of REM sleep while breastfeeding (International Childbirth Education Association 1969). Studies in animals have also shown that early abrupt weaning resulted in a prompt decrease in REM sleep rather than the more gradual change in sleep patterns seen with natural weaning.

### Mother and Baby Sleep Better

I have noticed how beautifully breastfeeding infants drift off to sleep and how they radiate a feeling of contentment during and following breastfeeding. I have also noticed that our babies would often fade out immediately after a breastfeeding as if they had been given a shot of a sleeping medication. Is it possible that there is an as-yet-undiscovered sleep-inducing substance in breast milk? In fact, researchers have found a sleep-inducing protein in human milk (Graf et al 1984).

*Breastfeeding relaxes both mother and baby.*

Breastfeeding helps mothers sleep. A mother told me that when she has trouble sleeping, she lies down with her baby and nurses him. In this case, the baby helps put the mom to sleep. This may be the result of the relaxing effect of prolactin. Observers report that in the postpartum period, breastfeeding has a sleep-inducing effect on the mother resulting in improved quality of post-feeding sleep (Bourne 1983).

## Medical Advantages
One of the advantages of night nursing to the mother is that it helps prevent breast infections. Mothers who practice night nursing become less engorged and suffer fewer breast infections in the early months because the breast is not allowed to become too full. When a mother who has become accustomed to the practice of night nursing encounters an uninterrupted night's sleep, she usually awakens with uncomfortably full breasts. Engorgement with the risk of breast infection is a classic example of what happens when biological harmony is disrupted.

## Babies Grow Better
I have noticed that infants grow better when they sleep with their mothers and nurse frequently during the night. One of the oldest treatments for the slow gaining baby is to "take your baby to bed and nurse." Some mothers tell me that they experience a stronger let-down reflex at night. The more efficient let-down would give night nursers milk higher in fat and thus higher in the calories they need to grow. The increased skin-to-skin contact during night nursing may also have a beneficial effect on babies' growth.

Mothers' prolactin levels are higher when they are sleeping. Since prolactin is the primary hormone involved in milk production, the quantity of breast milk available should be greater when baby sucks at night. In cultures practicing unrestricted breastfeeding, studies have shown that infants obtain as many of their daily calories during the night as they do during the day (Jelliffe and Jelliffe 1978). Growth hormone is also secreted mostly at night in babies and children. If babies are meant to grow at night, they are surely meant to eat at night.

Research has found that breast milk contributes to better brain development in infants. Breast milk is higher than formula in the amino acid taurine, which promotes brain growth. Human milk also contains significant amounts of DHA and AA, fatty acids that provide material for building the sheath around nerve fibers that enables them to send messages. Higher blood levels of DHA and AA are associated with better visual and cognitive development in infants. Other studies have found evidence of higher IQs and better school performance in children who received human milk. So mother's milk is not only the best food for sleep, but the best food for thought as well.

## Night-Waking in Breastfed Infants

There is a difference in night-waking patterns between formula-fed and breastfed infants. Breast milk is digested more rapidly than formula, and formula-fed babies may feel full longer. A study comparing night-waking between breastfed and bottle-fed infants around six months of age showed that 52 percent of breastfed babies awakened during the night compared to 20 percent of bottle-fed babies. This study also showed that of those infants who continued nursing until twelve months or more, 67 percent showed night-waking (Carey 1975). In this study, night-waking was defined as "waking and crying one or more times between midnight and 5:00 A.M. for at least four out of seven nights for at least four consecutive weeks between six and twelve months of age."

Why did breastfed infants wake more frequently at night? It is difficult to determine. The type of milk may not have been the main reason for these differences in night-waking. The mother's responsiveness to a waking and crying baby may have been a very important variable. In general, breastfeeding mothers show a less restrained response to their babies' crying. In an editorial comment about this study, Dr. Dana Raphael (1976), director of the Human Lactation Center in Westport, Connecticut, commented:

> There is implicit in the discussion of night-waking, the idea that something sacred and healthful will occur if the mother and the infant sleep eight straight-through hours. . . . I would suggest that the problem is in the

=== *When Help Isn't Help* ===

*"My mother has come to help with our new baby, our
first baby. She has offered to get up at night and give
the baby a bottle so that I can sleep and also to give
him a bottle occasionally during the day so that I can
get out. Is this all right? Will it interfere with breastfeeding?"*

Your mother means well and she is certainly trying to
mother you, the new mother. But this is an example of
exchanging an apparent short-term gain for a long-term
loss. In the first few weeks mothers and babies are trying
to develop a harmonious breastfeeding relationship. This
means (among other things) allowing the balance
between the mother's milk supply and the baby's demand
to develop without interference. Relief bottles in the first
few weeks definitely interfere with this. Sucking on an
artificial nipple is an entirely different action than sucking at the breast. Introducing another type of nipple at
the same time baby is learning to suck from your breast
may confuse him and slow his learning. Relief bottles can
cause breast engorgement because your breasts are not
being emptied frequently. Engorgement can trigger a
whole range of breastfeeding problems that will result
eventually in less rest for you. In the postpartum period,
your mother is there to take care of you and your household, not to be a substitute mother for your new baby.

This is going to take a little diplomacy on your part.
Because of your mother's love for her grandchild, she will
naturally want to help and advise. However, for the sake
of her grandchild, this help and advice should be on your
terms and not grandmother's. Grandmother has had her
shot at motherhood. Now it's your turn.

expectations and anxieties of our culture about sleep. . . .
I reckon the problem to be centered right in the middle
of an alarm clock. It certainly reflects a social system so
arranged that women have to be up to serve breakfast,
run all the household errands, clean, wash, cook, baby

tend, etc., without the support of others. These are the culprit facts which make night feeding a problem. The infant and mother have very little to do with it.

### Marathoning

"She wants to nurse all night" is a common and normal night-time concern among breastfeeding mothers. There may be several reasons for this kind of marathon nursing. In the first few months (usually around three weeks, six weeks, and three months), babies undergo several growth spurts when they nurse frequently all day and all night. This builds up the milk supply in response to the baby's increased nutritional needs.

Another reason for marathon nursing at night is that around the second or third month babies become more sensitive to visual stimuli. During the day they are distracted by all the visual delights of their newly discovered world. Your baby may suck a little and look a little, suck a little and look a little, and be unable to nurse very effectively during the day. At night, his world is not as visually stimulating. He is not as distracted (neither is his mother), and he settles down to catch up on his meals. Mother may feel like an all-night diner. If your tolerance level permits, I advise you to keep the diner open, because baby is doing what he needs to do. If your fatigue is becoming overwhelming, try the following to minimize visual distractions during the day. Nurse your baby in a darkened and uninteresting room, a trick called sheltered nursing. Siblings clamoring for attention may also be disturbing the little nurser.

## Tips for Night Nursing

### Releasing the Sleeping and Sucking Baby

Some babies like to sleep with the feeling of the nipple in their mouths. They don't relax their jaws even though they are sound asleep. They may release your nipple only after an hour or so. Occasionally a baby like this will hold on all night long. Some mothers learn to maintain this position quite comfortably and sleep attached throughout the night (or nap time). They're just thankful the baby is asleep. If you need to get up or can't sleep comfortably in this nursing position, you can learn to help the baby let go of the nipple without waking him from his deep sleep.

A baby may wake up when you disengage the nipple because he startles at the sudden loss of pressure in his mouth. If your baby stirs and wakes when you interrupt this pressure, experiment with more gradual ways of breaking the suction. One way is to insert a finger at the side of the baby's

mouth and gently pry his jaws open. As the jaws release, slowly draw the nipple out of his mouth. If you sense him stirring or groping for the nipple, he may be reacting to the change in pressure in his mouth. If you push firmly inward and upward just under his lower lip with the length of your index finger as you draw the nipple out, you can close his mouth firmly and apply just enough pressure to keep him from awakening. Hold the pressure with your finger until you sense your baby settle back to deep sleep. If he does arouse completely he will grope for your nipple with his mouth and hands. Quickly give the nipple back to him and try again after he has nursed his way back to a deep sleep. You may have to do this three or four times before he stays still, but it usually works on the first try if the baby is really in deep sleep and you have been patient enough not to rush it.

### Burping the Night Feeder

Develop a burping technique which keeps you and your baby in bed. Rather than getting out of bed and burping baby over your shoulder, continue lying on your side and allow baby to sit propped up against you as you apply pressure against his tummy. Babies do not need burping as much at night as during the day. Perhaps this is because they feed less anxiously at night and therefore swallow less air.

═══════ *The "Fill-'Em Up" Fallacy* ═══════

*"Our six-month-old-baby is awakening more often at night and seems really hungry. Does that mean it's time to start solids?"*

Most babies do not need solid food until six months (even later for some babies). If your baby's feeding interval becomes shorter around this age, this probably is a signal of increased nutritional requirements which can be met either by more frequent breastfeeding or by adding solid foods. If you increase the frequency of breastfeeding and your baby seems satisfied, then there is no need to begin solids. If however you don't wish to increase the frequency of feedings or your baby is not satisfied with only liquid nutrition, then he may indeed be ready for solids. Another sign of readiness is how your baby's tongue and swallowing movements respond to solid food. Try placing a tiny bit of very ripe mashed banana on the tip of your finger. Place the little bit of banana on your baby's tongue. If the tongue goes in, he's ready; if the tongue comes out, he's not. Stuffing your baby full of solid foods such as cereal before bedtime does not diminish night-waking.

### The Effect of "Filler Food" on Night-Waking

One of the long-standing remedies for prolonging sleep in infants is cereal before bedtime. This "fill the baby up with food" fallacy is an unwise feeding practice and may interfere with later appetite control. In fact, studies have shown that starting cereal early makes absolutely no difference in the length of sustained sleep, the frequency of night-waking, or the ratio of day to night sleep in infants at four months of age.

### Scheduled vs. Demand Feedings

With the advent of formula feeding, rigid four-hour feeding schedules were imposed on babies in the hope that they could be trained into a regular and predictable sleep-wake schedule. Studies have shown that feeding schedules or lack of schedules do not lessen a baby's frequency of night-waking (Parmlee 1964).

### *Nighttime Bottles*

In artificially fed babies, bottles may be used to induce sleep as part of the bedtime ritual or during the middle of the night. However, babies should not be allowed to continue nursing from the bottle after they have fallen asleep. When a baby falls asleep the amount of saliva decreases and its rinsing action is less effective. This allows the sugars from the formula (or juice) to bathe the teeth during the night. This may result in severe decay of the front teeth, a condition known as bottle-mouth caries. This dental problem very seldom occurs with breastfeeding. Bottle-fed babies should also be parented to sleep, which excludes bottle propping.

What about the baby who just won't part with his nighttime bottle of milk or juice? Some babies need to suck to sleep, even well into the second or third year. A useful trick that respects this nighttime need yet prevents bottle-mouth dental caries is called "watering down." Dilute the juice or milk with water, increasing the proportion of water night by night. After a few weeks the bottle will contain almost all water.

## Foods That Can Interfere with Baby's Sleep

### *Caffeine*

There is marked variability in individual sensitivity to the effects of caffeine. Caffeine interferes with sleep a great deal in some people and very little in others. Caffeine passes through the milk of the breastfeeding mother and may disturb the sleep and behavior of her baby. Caffeine enters breast milk in very small amounts, so that a breastfeeding mother would have to ingest a lot of caffeine (at least six cups of coffee) in order to notice an effect in her infant. Again, there is a marked variability in mothers' and babies' sensitivity to caffeine. Caffeine usually prolongs the time needed to fall asleep and disrupts the normal sleep stages. Persons quitting caffeine after heavy use may experience withdrawal headaches and feel less alert and more irritable. Caffeine-containing foods include coffee, colas, tea, and chocolate. Breastfeeding mothers should be aware that some over-the-counter drugs, including cold and headache remedies and diet pills, contain significant amounts of caffeine. Be sure to check the label if your baby is caffeine sensitive.

### Nicotine

Smokers usually take longer to fall asleep and are awake more during the night, an effect similar to that of caffeine. Studies have shown that smoking may suppress prolactin levels in breastfeeding mothers, especially those smoking more than fifteen cigarettes per day (Nybor 1982). Smoking has also been linked to earlier weaning and lower milk production.

### Alcohol

A small amount of alcohol, such as a glass of wine, may help a person get off to sleep sooner and have little detrimental effect throughout the rest of the night, but heavy drinking before bedtime takes its toll in the second half of the night. A person may go to sleep more quickly and appear to be in a stupor, but the effects of the alcohol wear off, causing the sleeper to sleep less soundly and to wake up earlier, with the symptoms of a hangover: dry mouth, aching muscles, throbbing head, and pounding heart. Alcohol generally suppresses REM sleep. Chronic alcoholics frequently experience nightmares, and these are intensified during alcohol withdrawal. In general, excessive alcohol disturbs rather than improves sleep.

### Junk Foods

Foods high in cane sugar and artificial coloring may interfere with sleep. Some children are more vulnerable to the effects of junk food than others. In response to highly sugared and highly colored foods, many children show diminished attention spans, poor school performance, mood swings, and sleep disturbances.

Rebound hypoglycemia can disturb sleep. If a high sugar meal is eaten before bedtime, a child's blood sugar is very high when he goes off to sleep. This high blood sugar triggers an excessive release of insulin which may cause the blood sugar to fall very rapidly to low levels during the night. The brain is highly dependent on an adequate supply of blood sugar for fuel, and when the blood sugar drops to low levels, a sleep disturbance may result.

The best kind of sugars for children are the natural sugars in milk products (unless the child is allergic to milk) and in fruit; the sugar in fruit, fructose, does not cause this rebound hypoglycemia. For this reason, bedtime snacks of fruit are less likely to cause sleep disturbances than candy bars. Fructose sugars (honey, unsweetened frozen juice concentrates) can be used as sweeteners instead of table sugar, especially in baking and cooking. (Honey should not be given to babies under one year of age.)

## Foods That Improve Sleep

An effective sleep inducer which has received a lot of attention in the popular press is L-tryptophan. This is not a drug but a naturally occurring amino acid found within the body and in many foods. The average person consumes one to two grams of tryptophan in food each day. Cheese, milk, pork, veal, and eggs are high in tryptophan. Tryptophan is now extracted from foods and is available in health food stores and pharmacies. It is thought to induce sleep when the body converts it into a chemical called serotonin which is found in high concentrations in the brain and is thought to be critical for sleep.

Tryptophan may turn out to be nature's own sleeping pill. Studies have shown that one gram of tryptophan taken forty-five minutes before you want to fall asleep can markedly reduce the time it takes to fall asleep. Tryptophan does not appear to affect sleep stages adversely or have a hangover effect the following day like many sleeping pills do. It appears to be safe and effective as a natural sleep inducer in adults, and the only apparent side effects recorded to date are nausea and vomiting following the use of high doses. Parents should check with their physician before taking tryptophan supplements.

### A Proper Bedtime Snack

The best bedtime snacks are foods which are high in tryptophan and contain some calcium along with healthy carbohydrates (fruits and whole grains). The carbohydrates and calcium make the tryptophan more effective. Sticky sugars (honey, caramel, syrup, raisins) should not be given to a child before bedtime because they promote dental caries. They stay in contact with the teeth longer, and the rinsing action of saliva is less during sleep. Suggested bedtime snacks are:

*A glass of warm milk*
*(for children who are no longer nursing)*

*Cheese and crackers*

*A bowl of cereal with fruit*

*Naturally sweetened ice cream*

*Peanut butter sandwich*

*Yogurt with fruit*

*Yogurt and whole grain cereal*

Keep in mind that the stomach should neither be too full nor too empty when approaching sleep.

## References

Bourne, M. 1983. The sleep of a mother after birth. *Midwives Chron* August, p. 27.

Carey, W. B. 1975. Breastfeeding and night waking. *J Pediatr* 87:327.

Graf, M. V. et al. 1984. Presence of delta-sleep-inducing peptide-like material in human milk. *J Clin Endocrinol Metab* 59:127.

Hofer, M. 1982. Some thoughts on "The transduction of experience" from a developmental perspective. *Psychosom Med* 44:19.

Hofer, M. and Shair, H. 1982. Control of sleep-wake states in the infant rat by features of the mother-infant relationship. *Dev Psychobiol* 15:229.

International Childbirth Education Association. 1969. *ICEA News* 8(1):4.

Hopkinson, J. et al. 1992. Milk production by mothers of premature infants: Influence of cigarette smoking. *Pediatrics* 90:934.

Jelliffe, D. B. and Jelliffe, E. F. P. 1978. *Human Milk in the Modern World*. Oxford: Oxford University Press.

Mansbach, I. et al. 1991. Onset and duration of breastfeeding among Israeli mothers: Relationships with smoking and type of delivery. *Soc Sci Med* 33:1391.

Lucas, A. et al. 1992. Breast milk and subsequent intelligence quotient in children born preterm. *Lancet* 339:261.

Nybor, A. et al. 1982. Suppressed prolactin levels in cigarette smoking breastfeeding women. *Clin Endocrinol* 17:363.

Parmlee, A. 1964. Infant sleep patterns: from birth to 16 weeks of age. *Pediatrics* 65:576.

Raphael, D. 1976. Night waking: a normal response? *J Pediatr* 88:169.

Rogan, W. et al. 1993. Breastfeeding and cognitive development. *Early Hum Dev* 31:181.

# Chapter 7

# Causes of Night-Waking in Infants and Children

By now you realize that night-waking in children is inevitable. It's not easy for parents to endure, but night-waking is difficult for babies, too. Fortunately there are some causes of night-waking over which you have some control. In this chapter we will explore the emotional, physical, environmental, and medical reasons why your child may wake up.

## Emotional Causes of Night-Waking

In the first year or two most of the emotional causes of night-waking are due to separation anxiety. Not until sometime around age three does the child develop the ability to comprehend that when mother and father are out of sight they continue to exist and will return.

Sometimes an infant who is weaned from his parents' bed into separate quarters before he is ready will begin waking up frequently. The child's previous nighttime harmony has been disrupted. He may not realize that mother and father are around the corner in another room. He is now out of harmony with his nighttime environment, and separation anxiety appears, leading to frequent night-waking. Reestablishing the conditions which caused the previous harmony usually corrects this problem.

Fears, nightmares, and disturbing dreams are the most common emotional causes of night-waking in the child over two. Children often distort reality in their dreams; the friendly neighborhood dog may appear as a monster. The dreams of young children are often reenactments of daytime experiences. You can expect more night-waking when your family's usual routines are upset by both pleasant and unpleasant events. Parents can influence dream content in their young child by minimizing exposure to disturbing visual influences during the day, for example, violence and fantasy on television. Don't underestimate the influence of television programs on the child's subconscious.

Anticipate more sleep disturbances if there is some disturbance in the total family harmony such as separation, divorce, illness, or family strife. This is especially true in homes in which harmony previously existed. When one family member is disturbed, the entire family unit is affected. Sleep problems are particularly common in young boys following some separation from father, a situation called father hunger. During domestic crises some children cling more tenaciously to wakefulness; others sleep more as a way of withdrawing from a situation they can't understand or handle. In custody and visitation squabbles, sleep problems are particularly frequent if a baby is required to sleep away from mother prior to weaning.

## Physical Causes of Night-Waking

### Your Baby May be Hungry
Tiny babies have tiny tummies, about the size of their tiny fists. A baby's digestive system is designed for small frequent feedings, so expect your baby to need a feeding at least every two to three hours around the clock for the first few months.

### Baby Is Wet
Most babies get used to an occasional feeling of wetness and therefore are not bothered by this. If you are using cloth diapers, putting two diapers on your baby before bedtime may help to minimize the discomfort of wetness.

### Baby Is Too Cold or Too Hot

As a general rule, dress and cover your baby in as much or as little clothing as you would wear yourself. Add one more layer for the baby who is premature, weighs under ten pounds, or has little insulating body fat. Cotton clothing is best because it absorbs body moisture and allows air to circulate freely. Clothing should be loose enough to allow free movement. Check periodically to see that the feet on your baby's sleepers are not too tight. Some tiny babies have cold feet, necessitating socks at night.

### Your Baby May Be Teething

Teething pain often accounts for frequent night-waking in babies between five and seven months who previously settled well. Although you may not actually feel or see your baby's teeth until six or eight months, teething discomfort may start as early as four months and is accompanied by profuse drooling. A wet bedsheet under his head and a drool rash on his cheeks and chin where he rubbed his face against the wet sheets are signs that your baby may be teething. Teething can continue to be a problem as additional teeth appear all the way through the two-year molars. (For more information about teething, see "Temporary Night-Waking and Teething" on the next page.)

### Developmental Milestones

Your baby may be practicing a new developmental skill even while he sleeps. Motions like grabbing, crawling, pushing up, or rolling over may wake him.

## Environmental Causes

### Temperature Too Hot or Too Cold

The consistency of the temperature in your baby's room is as important or even more important than the actual temperature. Premature or small babies under five-and-one-half pounds have incompletely developed temperature-regulating systems at birth and need a reasonably consistent temperature to avoid cold

# Temporary Night-Waking and Teething

*"Our six-month-old baby is such a good baby. He usually sleeps through the night, but even if he does awaken once or twice to nurse, he settles back to sleep very easily in his own bed. However, in the last few weeks, he is awakening more often and sometimes it takes me an hour to get him back to sleep. Could it be his teeth?"*

The period from four to six months is usually a very stuffy or congested stage. A baby's saliva production increases in preparation for teething. This profuse saliva collects in the back of the throat, upsetting and awakening the baby. This is not really a cold but simply a mechanical nuisance. The mucus is too far back in the baby's nose and throat to get out easily, and parents feel frustrated when they try to relieve their baby's discomfort.

Babies can also awaken because of the pain associated with the teeth expanding into the gum or erupting through it. Teething pain (or any other type of pressure discomfort) is not easily alleviated and is an intense arousal stimulus which may awaken baby from a stage of deep sleep. This is upsetting and causes difficulty. There are some things you can do when your baby is teething. Give an appropriate dosage of acetaminophen when your infant goes to bed and again when he awakens if the interval has been at least three hours. Because it may take a lot longer to resettle a night-waker in this situation, be ready to go through your usual parenting-to-sleep routines. Expect a bit of shift work and shared parenting. On the first shift dad gets up with baby and paces and rocks; the next time, mom gets up with baby.

Sometimes night-waking is not so temporary, and a baby does not resettle into his previous sleep patterns even after a few nights of comforting measures. In this case, the painful arousal stimulus may have intensified your baby's anxiety about being separated from you. You may have to reassess your baby's sleeping arrangements and nighttime routines and readjust your expectations.

stress. Full-term healthy babies over eight pounds have enough body fat and their temperature-regulating systems are mature enough to feel comfortable in an environment similar to that of the average adult. Since babies do not adjust to marked swings in room temperature in the first few weeks, a consistent room temperature around 68 to 70 degrees Fahrenheit (21 degrees Centigrade) is preferable.

The relative humidity is an equally important feature in the baby's environment. Babies are most comfortable in an environment of circulating air with a humidity of at least 50 percent. Humidity helps maintain the consistency of the temperature. Dry air may also lead to nasal stuffiness in a baby's already narrow nasal passages. I recommend that you use either a humidifier or a vaporizer in the room where your baby sleeps, especially during the winter months of central heating. Clean the vaporizer weekly to remove allergens such as mold. When traveling with a tiny baby, it is wise to take along a vaporizer during the winter months, especially if you are staying in motels or cabins with electric heat.

### Environmental Irritants

Substances in the air may contribute to nasal stuffiness and irritated eyes and awaken baby. Avoid exposing your baby to cigarette smoke, baby powder, fumes from paint, perfumes, hair spray, and lint from clothing. Wash baby clothing and bed clothing before using them. The most common nasal irritant that contributes to sniffles is cigarette smoke. I strongly advise parents to make "no smoking" a household rule when there is a baby in the house.

### Noises

During the first few months, the tiny baby is more easily aroused by noise than by light or touch. The predominance of REM sleep (a more active or aware state of sleep) and the more frequent cycling from REM to non-REM probably account for the increased arousal because of environmental stimuli during the first few months. As a general guide, the more consistent the environmental noise, the less likely this noise will awaken the baby. The more similar the baby's environmental noises are to womb sounds, the less these noises will bother the baby. With increasing maturity, usually after four months, a baby's arousal because of environmental noises lessens.

# Medical Causes

## *Stuffy Nose*
Babies have narrow nasal passages and are nose breathers, so the slightest amount of nasal congestion can bother them. Some causes of nasal congestion are listed above under environmental irritants. Since your baby is too young to blow his own nose effectively, the following nose care tips can help reduce stuffiness. Prepare some nose drops with a pinch of salt in a glass of water (no more than a quarter-teaspoon salt to eight ounces of water). With a plastic eye-dropper, squirt a few drops into each nostril. These drops loosen the secretions and may stimulate your baby to cough or sneeze, which are his own protective mechanisms for clearing his breathing passages. Next, take a rubber bulb syringe (a nasal aspirator available at any drug store) and gently suck out the loosened secretions. Most babies protest at this intrusion into their nose. Using a humidifier or vaporizer and avoiding exposure to nasal irritants or allergens will help keep your baby's nose clear, thereby improving your baby's ability to settle.

## *Allergies*
In addition to environmental irritants, allergies, especially to substances in the environment in which your baby sleeps, can increase nasal and respiratory secretions and interfere with sleep. The most common respiratory allergens that your baby is likely to encounter are: cigarette smoke, house dust, cow's milk products, perfumes, hair sprays, animal dander (keep animals out of a child's bedroom), plants, clothing (especially wool), stuffed animals, feather pillows, blankets, and fuzzy toys that collect dust.

Telltale signs that your baby is allergic to something in his sleep environment are a clear runny discharge from his nose or eyes, sniffles, or persistent nasal congestion when he awakens. Eliminating potential allergens from your child's bed and bedroom will help him sleep better.

Food allergies may also be a cause of night-waking. A baby who is restless most of the night or who awakens with sudden colicky pains and a tense, gas-filled abdomen may be reacting to food in his breastfeeding mother's diet, or to something in his own diet. This baby may have other allergic symptoms as well, including colic, fussiness, rashes, and chronic ear infections or respiratory symptoms. The mother needs to eliminate the offending foods from her diet. Cow's milk is the most common culprit. She should avoid all dairy products and other foods that may include milk, cheese, or milk proteins. This may require careful reading of labels. Some babies are quite sensitive. Other possible allergens include eggs, wheat, citrus fruits, corn, onion, fish, peanuts, cabbage, chocolate, and other nuts.

### Gastroesophageal Reflux

Night-waking may also be related to episodes of gastro-esophageal reflux (GER), the regurgitating of stomach acids into the esophagus, the tube that leads from the mouth to the stomach. This can be quite painful for babies, similar to heartburn in adults. It may happen more easily when a baby is in a horizontal position, and thus can be a cause of night-waking. There are a number of other symptoms associated with GER, including frequent bouts of painful crying, spitting up after feeding, abdominal pain, fussiness after eating, and frequent respiratory infections.

Keeping baby in an upright position for thirty minutes after feeding can lessen GER symptoms. Smaller, more frequent feedings may also help. Studies show that GER is less severe in breastfed babies. Your doctor may have other suggestions to help your baby feel better until he outgrows this problem.

### Fever

Expect children to awaken during fever-producing illnesses. Many viruses produce a higher fever at night than during the day. Giving your child fever-lowering medicines during an illness or even during a teething period may lessen the temperature swings during the night. If your child has a fever-producing illness during the day, it is usually wise to give him the appropriate dosage of fever-lowering medications before bedtime in anticipation of the fever going up at night—even though he may appear to have a normal temperature before going to bed. It is usually unwise to awaken a sleeping child to take his temperature; just feel or kiss his forehead.

### Ear Infections

One of the more common causes of night-waking in the young child is an ear infection. I give my patients "Dr. Bill's Rule" for recognizing when a common cold has become an ear infection:

1.  *When the discharge from your child's nose changes from clear and watery to thick and yellow (a runny nose becomes a snotty nose).*

2.  *When your child has a cold plus yellow drainage from his eyes.*

3.  *When your child's personality during a cold changes from happy to cranky and he sleeps less well.*

These are signs that your child's cold has most likely progressed into an ear infection, and immediate medical attention should be obtained.

Sometimes a child with an ear infection will awaken frequently during the night but seems better during the day. Don't interpret this as a sign that the infection is improving. Take your child to the doctor the next day anyway. Ear infections bother a child more at night. When a child is lying down, the fluid from the infection presses on the eardrum. When he sits upright, the fluid drains away from the eardrum and there is less pressure. Infants with ear infections sit up or stand up in their crib at night, and mothers relate, "She seems better when I hold her, but I just can't put her down."

The danger of ear infection is also one of the reasons why babies should not be put down to sleep with a bottle. Lying down with a bottle predisposes the middle ear to infection. Unless a baby is particularly prone to recurrent ear infections, breastfeeding while lying down does not appear to cause ear problems.

## Worms

Pinworms look like tiny pieces of white thread about a third of an inch long. The pregnant female pinworm travels down the intestines and out the rectum to lay her eggs. This activity results in intense itching which often causes the child to awaken and scratch the egg-infested area around his anus and buttocks. These eggs are picked up under the fingernails and transmitted back into the child's mouth as well as to playmates and other members of the household. The swallowed eggs hatch in the intestines, mature, mate, and repeat the life cycle.

Itching symptoms and scratch marks around your child's anus suggest that he may have pinworms. Sometimes the tiny worms can be seen at night in the dark if you spread your child's buttocks and shine a flashlight on the anus. If you cannot see the worms but you still suspect they're there, place a piece of tape sticky side out on a popsicle stick or tongue blade and capture the eggs by pressing the sticky side of the tape against the anus. The tape test is best performed immediately when your child awakens, before his bath or bowel movement. Take the tape to your doctor where it can be examined under a microscope for pinworm eggs and treatment can be prescribed.

## Urinary Tract Infections

The smaller the child the less obvious the symptoms of urinary tract infections. If your baby is simply not doing well (not gaining weight properly, a change in sleeping habits, recurrent unexplained fevers, unexplained abdominal pain, vomiting and diarrhea, not growing normally, unexplained fatigue), he should have a proper urinalysis by your doctor. Urinary tract infections are great masqueraders.

## Pain at Night

As a general rule, pain which awakens a child at night is a greater concern than pain occurring during the day, and medical attention should be obtained. Also, parents should bear in mind that night pains are less likely to have a psychological origin than daytime pains. Pain is the body's alarm system that signals when something is not right. Responding to your child's nighttime pain is one of the most important parts of nighttime parenting.

## The Persistent Night-Waker

Frequent night-waking is a common, healthy behavior in newborns, but older babies and toddlers should be able to sleep longer stretches at night. Some children, however, who sleep next to their mothers are perfectly happy to nurse all night long. Some mothers can cope with this side-effect of sleep-sharing, but others find that they can't get enough rest when their child wakes them up many times each night.

I encounter mothers in my practice whose toddlers are waking up every hour all night long to nurse. Mother is tired and cranky, and although she wants to be sensitive to her child's nighttime needs, her lack of sleep is making it increasingly difficult to be the kind of parent she wants to be during the day. When your child's night-waking habits begin to affect your daytime parenting, it's time to take a realistic look at the situation and figure out what you can cope with and what you need to change.

The first step in solving the problem is to consider possible physical causes for the child's wakefulness. Frequent night-waking may be related to problems with food intolerance or allergy. Eliminating dairy foods and other common allergens from the diet of both mother and child sometimes improves the sleep situation.

Some older babies and toddlers nurse frequently at night because they (and their mothers) are too busy to nurse well during the day. Longer and more frequent nursing sessions during the day may help to cut down on the nighttime breastfeeding. You may have to nurse your child in quiet, dimly lit surroundings to minimize distractions and encourage her to nurse longer. Use this time to rest or sleep yourself if you are feeling tired and irritable. Also, spend plenty of time with your child in non-nursing activities during the day. This may decrease his need to demand attention in the middle of the night.

Babies and toddlers often wake more frequently during an illness or when they are entering a new developmental stage. Sometimes the night-waking persists even after the developmental challenge is mastered or the child has gotten over the illness or the allergy symptoms. The child gets in the habit of waking frequently at night, and eventually mother becomes exhausted and resentful. At this point, parents need to take some action. Here are some suggestions.

### Fill His Tummy
When your child awakens to nurse at night, sit up in bed with him and be sure he nurses well for ten to fifteen minutes. If he nurses for only the few minutes it takes to put himself back to sleep, he'll soon be awake and hungry again.

### Put Some Distance between You
A child who is sleeping nestled against your breast is likely to seek the nipple anytime he stirs in his sleep. Try nursing the child to sleep on a mattress on the floor next to your bed. When he awakens at night, you can move down to the floor to nurse him and then return to your bed. Many children awaken less often when mother is not quite so close.

### Teach Other Ways to Fall Asleep
Begin to teach your child other ways to fall asleep besides nursing. Nurse him until he is relaxed and drowsy, but then take him off the breast and pat his back, rock him, or just snuggle with him until he is asleep. When he awakens at night, mom or dad can try one of these alternatives instead of nursing. You may be able to resettle him quickly before he is fully awake and demanding to nurse. Gradually he'll learn to relax back to sleep on his own.

### Rules for Nighttime Nursing
An older toddler or preschooler should be able to accept some limits on nighttime nursing. Talk about these during the day for several days before they go into effect. Say "We nurse at bedtime, and then we don't nurse again until the sun comes up" or "We don't nurse until Daddy wakes up and gets out of bed." When the child awakens at night, you remind him of the

rules, comfort him if he is upset, perhaps offer a drink of water, but you don't nurse him. Your child may protest this new arrangement and you may have a few rough nights, but most children soon learn to wake up less often and to go back to sleep without nursing.

### "Father Nursing"

If mother is exhausted from nighttime nursing, it's time for dad to step in. When a child wakes up for the third or fourth or fifth time in as many hours, it's father's turn to do the comforting. He can soothe the night-waker by walking him, rocking him, patting him on the back, or whatever works. Letting dad take over may be necessary if the mother can no longer cope well during the day because of not sleeping at night. This solution can be difficult for a sensitive, attached mother to accept, but she should remember that having dad comfort the baby is not the same as "letting him cry." Crying in the arms of a familiar, well loved parent is not the same as being left alone behind the bars of a crib to "cry it out." Dad will need to be patient as his little one learns to accept this new way of being soothed. The payoff is that the child will learn that he can depend on father as well as mother to care for his needs.

It might be best to try this approach on a weekend, when dad does not not have to get up for work the next morning. If mother can't sleep when the baby is crying, either she or dad and the baby can go to a different room, out of earshot.

# Chapter 8

# Nighttime Parenting of the High Need Baby

One of the "for better or for worse" aspects of nighttime parenting is that so-called easy babies settle better than difficult babies. A baby's sleep pattern usually reflects his basic temperament. Easy babies seem to enjoy more deep sleep, whereas difficult babies often carry their waking personalities into their sleep.

Exhausting babies go by various names: the fussy baby, the difficult baby, the colicky baby, and the demanding baby. As these babies grow older they acquire labels such as the "terrible twos," the hyperactive child, the strong-willed child. I prefer to call this baby and child **the high need child.** This is a kinder term and it more appropriately expresses what these children are really like and the type of parenting they need. High need children also need a higher degree of nighttime parenting.

## Identifying High Need Children

You can spot these high need babies very early in infancy. These are the babies whose mothers just can't put them down. These are the babies who are inconsistently appeased; what works one day does not work the next. This is the child who continually challenges the ingenuity of the parents. One mother confided, "Just when I think I have the game won, she ups the ante." This type of child challenges the creativity of the teacher just as he does that of his parents. He often receives unfair labels such as hyperactive or learning disabled, which are often a sign of the mismatch between the child's needs and the school system. This child needs above-average teaching just as he needs above-average parenting. He does not adapt well to any average system, and if forced to, he becomes frustrated and bored, while his behavior deteriorates and becomes increasingly undesirable.

The high-need baby is intense, super-sensitive, often fussy and has prolonged periods of seemingly purposeless crying which interfere with sleep, feeding, and settling. He demands constant physical contact. He is often discontented and responds inconsistently to the usual modes of comforting. He is a time-consuming, energy-draining baby who sometimes elicits negative feelings in his mother, puts a strain on his parents' marriage, and produces anxiety and fatigue in the whole family, including himself.

Studies have confirmed a correlation between infant temperament and sleep patterns. In these studies easy babies were defined as regular, adaptable, approachable, and positive in mood; difficult babies were irregular, low in adaptability and acceptance of an initial approach, intense, and negative. The researchers found that difficult babies slept about two hours less each night and one hour less during the day than the easy babies did. Babies who exhibit a very active temperament during the day usually have a higher degree of restless and squirming activity while sleeping.

## Sleep Problems in High Need Children

A tired mother once asked me, "Why do high need babies need more of everything but sleep?" This seems to be an apparent mismatch between temperament and sleep needs. It may seem that high need children should need more sleep. (Their exhausted parents do.) I feel that these babies are more prone to sleep problems because of two causes, a different level of adaptability and a less effective stimulus barrier.

## Adaptability

Early on, many babies fuss because of their inability to adjust to life outside the womb. They just don't feel right. They miss the womb. Consider the secure and constant world of the fetus in utero. He is in constant motion, constant touch, surrounded by a consistent temperature. His needs are consistently and automatically met. His feeding is continuous, and most of the sounds of his environment are rhythmic. The unborn infant is in harmony with his environment. Any changes in the womb are gradual. Then comes birth. The changes at birth and during the postpartum period are abrupt. Life outside the womb is not so secure, and the response to his needs will never again be as automatic or predictable.

A contented baby experiences his environment as right. He can adjust easily to change, seek pleasurable experiences, and adapt to unpleasant experiences. The fussy baby does not feel content; he does not feel right. He is unable to adapt to postnatal life yet has an intense desire to be comfortable. This conflict between wanting comfort and not being able to achieve it results in fussy behavior.

## The Stimulus Barrier

Another reason why babies fuss involves what is called a stimulus barrier. The stimulus barrier allows babies to receive pleasant stimuli and block out unpleasant stimuli. This is part of a baby's adaptation to postnatal life. You will notice that some babies tune out unpleasant noises or pain by falling asleep. This stimulus barrier matures faster and to a greater degree in some babies than in others. Fussy babies' stimulus barriers seem to be more permeable, causing them to be more sensitive.

Sleep researchers refer to the effectiveness of the stimulus barrier as the **sensory threshold,** the level of stimulation that is necessary to invoke a discernible response. In simple language, the sensory threshold indicates how much you have to bother a baby in order to get a reaction. If a baby reacts intensely to very little stimulation, he is said to have a low sensory threshold; if a baby reacts very little to a lot of stimulation he is said to have a high sensory threshold, that is, a strong stimulus

# The Wide-Awake Newborn

*"I thought newborns just slept and ate. All mine does is eat. We have been home from the hospital three days and I haven't had a decent night's sleep yet. She wants to be held constantly during the day, she naps very infrequently, and she nurses every few hours through the night. I am exhausted. I need help."*

You may not have one of those "average" newborns who sleeps eighteen hours a day and awakens only a couple of times at night. You have an above-average child who needs above-average parenting. The earlier that you recognize this and develop realistic expectations of your baby's behavior and your own ability to cope, the more you will enjoy your child.

Talk with your husband and discuss your baby's needs together. Encourage him to read parts of this book. The high need baby needs two highly involved parents. Dad has no choice in this matter; baby needs shared parenting. Get help with the housework: your mother, mother-in-law, or anyone who can cook and can clean house.

Define priorities. You don't have to be the perfect wife, housekeeper, social chairman, and the perfect mother. For the first months, you are still on maternity leave from all of these other obligations. Stick to one thing—mothering your baby. When your baby's needs begin to decrease and your energies are on the rise, you can resume some of these other commitments.

Sleep with your baby. Nap when your baby naps and welcome her into your bed at night. Your baby may be very resistant to any form of manipulation of her sleep patterns. In the first few weeks it will be easier for you to adjust to your baby's sleep patterns than to try to get your baby to conform to yours. As your baby gets older her sleep patterns will become more organized. Surround yourself with positive supportive people who can encourage you on down days.

barrier. Studies have shown that infants with low sensory thresholds wake many times at night, whereas infants with high sensory thresholds wake less often.

Infants and young children are more susceptible to night-waking. As a child gets older, the number of vulnerable periods for awakening lessens. This sleep maturity seems to take longer to develop in high need children. These children are very sensitive to environmental stimuli by day and carry this sensitivity into their sleep patterns at night. Parents of a high need child will often describe him as "exhausting but bright." These children seem to be constantly awake and aware, by day and by night, as though they possess an internal light bulb that is always on. Their inner radar system is always tuned in and processing the stimuli around them. One of the problems is that these children never want to turn the light off or the radar down. They do not easily detach themselves from the delights of their environment. They do not give up easily and are therefore very difficult to get to sleep. A 7:00 P.M. bedtime is usually an unrealistic expectation for these children. Some sleep researchers feel that it is the **ability to stay awake** that reflects the maturation of the brain, rather than the ability to go to sleep or sleep through the night.

# Surviving and Thriving with Your High Need Child

Because most of the characteristics of the high need child stem from his own inborn temperament, his slow adaptation to life outside the womb, his immature stimulus barrier, and his high level of awareness, successful nighttime parenting of this child involves sensitivity to all of these areas.

### *Arrange to Keep Your Baby with You from the Moment of Birth*
Provide a smooth transition from the womb to the outside world. No matter what birth options you choose, unless some medical complication exists, plan on rooming-in with your baby. Babies who room-in with their mothers cry less at night and organize their sleep patterns more quickly than babies

cared for in a central nursery. This period of mother-infant bonding extends the harmony that your infant enjoyed within your womb, an unsurpassed feeling of rightness that can only be given by a caregiver whom he has already known for nine months. Anthropologist Ashley Montagu appropriately describes the rooming-in arrangement as a "womb with a view" (1978).

At this point, let me give a world of encouragement to those mothers who for some reason, cannot have their babies with them in the hours after birth. Bonding is not like instant glue which at a critical time suddenly and irrevocably cements the mother-child relationship together forever. Bonding is a lifelong process of mother-child interaction. There is no evidence that missing this initial bonding period, for example, because of a cesarean birth, has a permanent effect on the mother-baby relationship. Immediate contact with the baby simply gives the relationship a head start and is an advantage to the high need child. Effects of necessary mother-baby separation can be minimized by having father stay with the baby until mother is available.

### Breastfeed Your Baby

The benefits of breastfeeding are particularly important for the high need child and his mother. The hormone prolactin, present in much higher amounts in breastfeeding mothers, has a relaxing effect. Certainly mothers of high need babies need all the help with relaxation that they can get. In addition, I strongly suspect that prolactin helps the mother increase her level of **acceptance,** which is absolutely necessary for nighttime parenting of this type of child. The hormone prolactin is usually referred to as the mothering hormone. I have often considered prolactin to be a perseverance hormone also. In general, I have noticed that high need babies, if permitted, do tend to breastfeed more often during the day and night, and they wean at a later age.

### Don't Compare Babies

"Why can't I get more than three hours of uninterrupted sleep? Why doesn't my baby sleep like other babies?" complained a tired mother of a high need child. You don't have the other mother's baby, and the other mother may not have your parenting style. Don't compare. This leads to frustration and blaming yourself and contributes to early burnout. Follow the example of mothers of disabled children who have learned this important survival lesson: look at the child in relation to the child, not in comparison to others.

## Surround Yourself with Positive Friends and Support Groups

There is great comfort in knowing that your baby isn't the only baby in the whole wide world who fusses. I keep a list of parents who have survived the parenting of a fussy baby and often refer new parents of a fussy baby to the parents on my list. Keep in mind that fussiness is often in the eyes of the beholder. After meeting with parents who truly do have a fussy baby, the new parents often report, "We don't have a fussy baby after all."

One of the most effective support groups that I recommend to mothers of high need babies is La Leche League. Support groups such as this will help you develop a high level of understanding and acceptance of your baby. Support groups will also help a tired and frustrated mother work through some of her own ambivalent feelings. By talking with other mothers of fussy babies you will realize that it is normal to feel that "sometimes I don't like my baby" or "I'm being taken advantage of" or "I'm reaching the end of my rope." Supportive mothers will give you a tremendous sense of release by helping you understand that it's okay to have these feelings.

Avoid non-supportive and negative advice such as "Let your baby cry it out" and "Don't let him into your bed or you'll be sorry." These advisors give you the subtle message that your baby is fussing because of something you're doing or not doing. **Your baby fusses because of his own temperament and not because of your mothering abilities.** A fussy baby can shake the confidence of a new mother, and this can destroy many of the rewarding aspects of parenting. This leads to a vicious cycle: the less confident you are, the less effective you become at comforting your baby and the more inconsolable he becomes. This cycle often results in **escape mothering,** seeking alternative fulfillment such as a career or other activity outside the home that has more tangible immediate rewards. Avoid listening to these negative advisors (or becoming a negative advisor yourself). Most well-meaning advisors do not understand the concept of the high need child. It may help to explain why your child is a special child and why he needs a special style of parenting. In my practice I advise mothers to use me, the doctor, as a scapegoat. "Tell your mother-in-law that you are following your doctor's advice." This gets you off the hook.

**Slings, Swings, and Other Things Gentle the Fussy Baby.**
For some babies, stillness is the state in which they seem most relaxed. But most babies prefer motion and sound. Most fussy babies are calmed by three conditions: motion, sound, and physical contact, or "back to the womb" effects. Gentling the fussy baby works on the principle of competing behavior. This means that you are competing with your baby's own tense behavior by imposing your own gentling behavior. The art of comforting the fussy baby consists of determining what type of motion, sound, and physical contact your baby likes and needs and knowing how much you can give of yourself without exhausting your parental reserves. These babies usually are much more comfortable being carried around in slings or cloth baby carriers (front and side carriers in the first six months) which allow baby to nestle on mother's breast or father's chest and be comforted by the closeness and by the familiar rhythm of the heartbeat and the breathing motions. Try to carry your baby with as much skin-to-skin contact as possible. The combination of skin-to-skin touching (with your baby's ear over your heart) and your rhythmic breathing movements and total body rhythm will often soothe a fussy baby.

**Develop your own colic carries.** Listen to your baby and he will tell you what mode of transportation he likes best. The snuggling position that has worked best for our fussy baby was for me to place her chest against my chest. She gradually evolved a position with her head turned to one side and nestled under my chin, as if she figured out that this was the position of maximum skin-to-skin contact. As she got older, she would automatically assume this nesting position without any coaching on my part. Another effective colic carry is the football carry. Baby is draped stomach-down over your forearm with your hand firmly clasping the diaper area, legs astraddle, and head resting in the bend of your elbow.

Experiment with various colic carries until you find the style which most effectively calms your baby and induces quietness or sleep. The mothers and fathers of fussy babies whom I have watched seem to have developed a type of dance with their babies: a rhythmic swaying, waddling, or rocking motion accompanied by skin-to-skin caresses and lulling vocal sounds. After the parents have finished the ballet, the baby falls limp in their arms and melts into the harmony of this "back to the womb" activity.

**Call in the reserves.** Fussy babies need to be constantly in arms, but it does not always have to be the mother's arms. If you have exhausted your medley of colic carries and dances, your arms are wearing out, or you have fallen into the tense mother/tense baby cycle (see below), call in another dancer with a fresh set of arms.

Basically these gentling suggestions create harmony, a "back to the womb" feeling. Realistically, the "womb" sometimes wears out, and mother substitutes may occasionally be necessary. If a pair of substitute arms are not available, a mechanical baby swing can be useful in calming a fussy baby and inducing sleep, while allowing you a few minutes of needed rest. Additional soothers and suggestions on "back to the womb" activities are discussed in Chapter Four.

## Relaxation Techniques

A fussy baby can shatter the nerves of even a shatterproof mother. It is necessary that you learn to relax by whatever method works for you. Being held in tense arms can be very upsetting to a baby who is already very sensitive to tension. This is called the **tense mother/tense baby** syndrome. Here are some relaxation tips to help you and your baby enjoy each other.

**Take a warm bath together.** Fill the tub to just below your breast level. Lie back in the tub and let your baby partially float while you hold and nurse him. This ritual is especially good when you know the baby's tired but he just won't give up and go to sleep. Enjoying a spa or warm bath together is a great relaxation help. Avoid prolonged exposure at water temperature greater than 100 degrees Fahrenheit (38 degrees Centigrade).

**Enjoy nestle nursing.** The breast is usually the old standby for soothing the fussy baby, but sometimes even breastfeeding doesn't work. If your baby refuses your breast and does not stop fussing, he may be giving you cues that he wants to lie down with you in bed and nurse, tummy to tummy, snuggled in your arms and nestled into your breasts. I noticed this signal in our babies. When breastfeeding did not soothe our crying baby, Martha said many times, "She must want to lie down and nurse."

**Get outdoor exercise.** Even if you have to force yourself to do so, a walk in the park with the baby in a front carrier can be a relaxing daily ritual for a tense mother and fussy baby. It also gets you away from the sight of all those chores screaming to get done.

**Nap when your baby naps.** Often mothers use their baby's nap time to "finally get something done." When parenting a high need child, it is easier to adjust your sleeping patterns to your child's than to try to force your child into a predetermined sleep schedule. Some babies just don't nap much during the day; in fact, studies have shown that babies with more difficult temperaments do sleep less during the day (Carey 1974). Although baby may not appear to need a nap, mother certainly does. When your baby does reward you with a long-awaited nap, take the phone off the hook and have a private relaxing time doing something just for yourself, preferably taking a nap. This is not the time to catch up on household chores.

## Set Priorities and Share the Parenting

Most mothers become exhausted not so much because of their high need babies, but because they have tried to keep up with all of their outside activities and obligations. You can't be all things to all people, and if you have a high need baby many of your outside commitments simply must go during the first few months or years of mothering. During this extended maternity leave, you may have to resign from many of the outside activities which compete with your mothering energy. In the first few weeks and months, even household activities like cooking, cleaning, and laundry may have to be delegated to someone else so you can give all it takes to yourself and your baby.

If you have a high need baby, you will very quickly realize that your baby requires two parents. This is the time for sincere communication between parents, for dad to be sensitive when mother's reserves are wearing thin and to volunteer and say, "I'll take the baby. You go do something for yourself." Father can calm the fussy baby and give the mother a break by walking and dancing with the baby.

## *Welcome Your Baby into Your Bed*

Sleeping with your baby is particularly helpful for the high need child since it continues the harmony by night that you work so hard to achieve by day. Occasionally parents are dead on their feet at 10:00 P.M., but their toddler is still wound up and won't wind down. In this case, if your bedroom is child-proof, simply bring him into your room, close the door, and go to bed. When your toddler is ready, he'll crash, too. Provide his own mattress on the floor.

## *Respond Promptly to Your Baby's Cries*

How you respond to your baby's cries during the day is part of your training in responding appropriately to your baby's cries at night. In parenting your high need baby you will be constantly picking him up when he cries or holding him continuously so he won't cry. If this practice feels right to you and it soothes your baby, then do it. Your baby will not be spoiled if he is picked up so often. He is more apt to be spoiled if he is not picked up. Babies who receive a prompt response to their cries eventually cry less. A need that is met will go away; a need that is not met may change course a bit, but it does not go away.

### *Feed Your High Need Child Right*

High need children are more vulnerable to the behavioral effects of junk food. Avoid highly sugared and highly colored foods and behavior-changing foods such as those that contain caffeine. Provide frequent healthy snacks.

## How to Avoid Burnout in Parenting the High Need Child

Having a high need child is one of the risk factors for mother burnout. One dictionary defines burnout as "to stop burning from lack of fuel" as well as physical or emotional exhaustion from long-term stress. Even for the most caring and persevering mothers there will be times when you exhaust your reserves and both mind and body wave a red flag which says, "I can't cope anymore." Mothers share these feelings with me daily. Mother burnout should not be considered a weakness. In fact, burnout is more common in highly committed mothers who want to do a good job of parenting.

An important consideration in avoiding mother burnout is recognizing when there is a mismatch between temperament and tolerance level of baby and mother. Some mothers have very fussy babies, but they themselves have a very high tolerance level. Other mothers may have an easier baby but lower tolerance levels. If this mismatch exists in your family, realize this early in your mothering career and seek consultation before this problem has a snowballing effect on your enjoyment of your child, your self-esteem, and on your marriage. Ask your local La Leche League for names of counselors who will support your parenting values. These may be pediatricians, psychologists, family therapists, or lactation specialists. One persistent mother from a small town in Washington state tracked me down for some much needed advice about her child's night-waking. She wrote me a detailed letter describing the problem and requesting a phone consultation. She even sent a picture of her little night-waker. I was delighted to help.

## The Fussy Family

Having a high need child is usually a problem for the whole family. Realistically a high need child completely dominates the family for at least the first few years. (I use the term dominates in a positive way, in the sense of setting priorities, rather than implying a lack of discipline and authority in the home.) Parents who have defined their priorities and who successfully parent the high need child may find that there is often little energy left over for the needs of their spouses. It is absolutely vital to reserve some energy for your marriage relationship. The single best support system for a high need child is the environment of a stable and fulfilled marriage.

## Nighttime Parenting and Family Burnout

Studies have documented that sleep difficulties in children can often wreck family life and may be a contributing factor to child abuse and marriage break-up (Campbell 1981). Your child's sleep problem becomes a total family problem when the child's frequent night-waking exceeds your ability to cope. Occasionally I will se a mother who is trying to be the perfect nighttime parent, but she is so exhausted that her effectiveness as a daytime mother, wife, and person is greatly diminished. The mother simply does not have enough energy to be up with her child frequently at night and also to meet everyone's needs during the day. I find this a most difficult situation in which to counsel parents, and I usually start by saying, "You have a problem in which you're not going to like any of the solutions, but we must admit that something has to go. By trying to be the perfect nighttime parent, you're not able to be an effective daytime parent and the whole family is losing." Usually a complete overhaul of the entire family situation is required, plus the use of some nighttime discipline techniques which must be individualized to each family.

Parents of very fussy babies may have to make compromises to avoid burnout. An example is the case of the frequent night nurser. The baby awakens every hour or two and wants to nurse more for comfort than because of hunger. In general, if mother's reserves are able to cope with this, I strongly encourage her to keep nursing at night. But in the special situation where nighttime parenting is leading to burnout, the father can comfort the baby for a few nights with alternative gentling methods while the mother sleeps. This suggestion is usually very difficult for mother to accept and fathers to perform. As one mother confessed, "It's very hard for me not to respond to my baby when I know I have the means to comfort her."

Much of this chapter on the high need child pertains to the art of daytime parenting, but a thorough understanding of good daytime parenting carries over into your nighttime parenting. Parenting is the type of profession that does not have separate job descriptions for the daytime and nighttime shifts.

**References**

Busby, K. et al. 1981. Sleep patterns in hyperkinetic and normal children. *Sleep* 4:366.

Campbell, K. 1981. Association of the domestic set-up with sleeping difficulties in children under three years of age. *Med J Austr* 2:254.

Carey, W. 1974. Nightwaking and temperament in infancy. *J Pediatr* 84:756.

Montagu, A. 1978. *Touching: The Human Significance of the Skin.* New York: Harper.

Thomas, A. et al. 1968. *Temperament and Behavior Disorders in Children.* New York: University Press.

Weissbluth, M. 1981. Sleep duration and infant temperament. *J Pediatr* 99:817.

Weissbluth, M. 1982. Chinese-American infant temperament and sleep durations. *J Dev Behav Pediatr* 3:99.

Weissbluth, M. 1983. Sleep patterns, attention span, and infant temperament. *J Dev Behav Pediatr* 4:34.

# Chapter 9
# Nighttime Fathering

In the first couple of years babies have a strong biological attachment to and therefore a preference for their mothers. This is not to say that father has only a minor supportive role. The attachment style of parenting can be very draining upon a mother who has to go it alone. For this style of parenting to really work, it is absolutely necessary that father be consistently involved.

## Normal Father Feelings

In the first few months after the birth of a baby, many fathers experience ambivalent feelings about the way their previously uncomplicated marriage relationship has changed. The strong mother-infant attachment may bring out resentment on father's part. "All she does is nurse." "She's too attached; that baby is hanging on her all day and now she even wants to sleep with the baby." "We need some time together, we need to get away. I have needs too." These are normal feelings from sincere and caring, but confused fathers. Fathers, it will help if you can understand what is going on within the new mother during the first few months after the baby arrives.

### *Understanding How a Woman Changes after Birth*

Before giving birth a woman's reproductive hormones are at higher levels than her maternal hormones. After birth, levels of the maternal hormones increase and stay increased for at least six to nine months. Because of this postpartum hormonal change a woman's mothering instinct may temporarily take priority over her sexual drives. This hormonal attachment to the baby has survival benefits that help the young of the species develop to their fullest potential. A mother is programmed to be attached to her baby physically and emotionally.

Some mothers naturally have a stronger programming than others, and some mothers have to work at it more. But this instinctual urge to mother is present in various degrees in all new mothers. This does not mean that you are being displaced by your infant in your wife's affections, but rather that some of the energies which were previously directed toward you are now being directed toward your baby. In time, these energies will return to you, especially if you have been an involved and supportive father early in your baby's life (even in pregnancy). This may be called a season of marriage, a season to parent. If the harvest is tended properly, the season to be sexual will

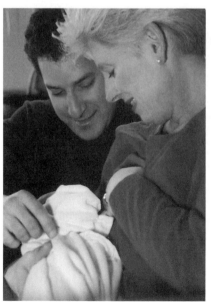

again return, and the marriage will mature.

Because of these hormonal changes and the fatigue that results from all the demands on the new mother, your wife may not be sexually responsive during the first few months after giving birth. Don't interpret this coolness to mean that she does not want to be sexually responsive or that she loves the baby more than you. It is simply that she is undergoing a whole series of emotional and physical changes and adjustments in her role as a mother. Mothers commonly attribute their lack of sexual drive to feeling "touched out," because of their continuing close contact with the baby. Fathers may have difficulty understanding these changes after birth. Although the new father does indeed have many adjustments of his own, he does not undergo any physical changes. It is also wise for mothers to understand that dad's hormones are the same before and after the birth.

## Is There Sex after Parenthood?

*Here are some tips for sexually frustrated fathers based on suggestions that worked for one young couple who asked my advice.*

Cathy and Jim were the parents of a baby who woke frequently during the night. Cathy especially put a lot of energy into caring for the baby, following the attachment style of parenting. When Jim wanted to have sex, Cathy was tired and uninterested. It wasn't that she was uninterested in Jim, but she was uninterested in sex.

When they talked to me about their problem, I suggested various nighttime parenting tips to help them cope with the baby's night-waking. I also suggested that Jim begin courting Cathy all over again. Little things would mean a lot: bringing her flowers, sending "I care for you" messages through eye contact, and touching. He could occasionally set the stage for a romantic evening by coming home, arranging a candlelight dinner, and taking care of the baby, freeing Cathy to relax.

I also encouraged Jim to be flexible. The best laid plans of lusty husbands can easily be foiled by a baby's unpredictable needs. If the baby awakens just as you are about to make love, avoid conveying a "curses, foiled again!" message. That will turn your wife off. Instead give her the message, "I'll help you tend to baby's needs and we'll make love later." For some reason, when a woman feels her husband is delaying his gratification in favor of their baby, she often feels more sexual.

Yes, there is sex after parenthood.

# A Matter of Trust

Because of the changes that occur in a new mother, it is necessary that dad trust mom's natural instincts. If mom wants to breastfeed on demand, sleep with the baby, and take the baby with her wherever she goes, trust that mother knows best. This trust relationship is also necessary for mom. It is vitally important that you trust your husband when he steps in and says, "What can I do to help?"

Another variable in mother-infant attachment is the level of your child's needs. Blessed with a high need child, a new mother may react in one of two ways, each eliciting a different reaction from dad. First, mother may increase her quality of mothering in proportion to the needs of the child. Father may interpret this increased attachment as behavior that is making the baby too dependent. This usually is not the case. Your wife is responding to your baby's need, not creating a habit. If you are confused about whether mom is causing your infant's behavior or responding to it, trust that she is responding. Second, a mother may sometimes feel inadequate to meet the child's needs. This may indicate a mismatch of temperaments, for example, a fussy baby and a mother with a low tolerance for fussing. This mismatch of needs and responses may bring about an increasing dependence upon dad to pitch in and help. Dad may feel equally unable to cope with the fussy situation. The following suggestions are aimed at helping fathers deal with these situations.

# Attachment Fathering Tips

### Be involved early

Involvement is the key for the new father with shaky father feelings. Ideally this involvement should start before the birth of your baby. Attending prepared childbirth classes will enable you to be involved in the birth of your baby. I have noticed that the earlier fathers are involved the more likely they are to stay involved.

During pregnancy and after the birth of your baby, practice "mothering the mother" as she mothers your baby. In most cultures a new mother is assigned a doula, usually another woman, who cares for her needs as she recovers from birth and adjusts to mothering. We don't have doulas in our culture, but dads can act as doulas to a certain extent. Free your wife of all household chores; they can be done by someone else. This releases her to do the one job no one else can do, mothering the baby. Get domestic help if you can afford it in the early weeks. Don't pressure your wife to function as housekeeper and social chairman. If your mother or mother-in-law comes to visit, be sure she is there to help with household tasks and not to be entertained. Be prepared to act as a buffer if any tensions develop.

Be involved in the care and enjoyment of your baby when you can: change diapers, bathe the baby, console him when he's fussy, play with him, etc. Not only does this give your wife a much-needed rest; it also helps you get to know your baby better. Increasing involvement in your baby's care will bring out your father's intuition, and you may be surprised how effective you really are. We talk so much about mother's intuition, and it is true that mothers have a biological edge over fathers in natural and intuitive baby care. I strongly believe that fathers have a bit of this nurturing intuition too, but it does not come as naturally. We have to work at it more. Appreciate that your wife may be reluctant to release the baby into your care at first. This is partly a natural protective instinct and partly a reflection of the cultural stereotype which portrays fathers as well-meaning but clumsy.

### Be supportive

Your wife's intuitive biological instincts to mother are very strong, but her confidence may be a bit shaky. A new mother's confidence needs periodic boosts, and ideally this should come from dad. Your job is constantly to give her the message, "Do what you feel you need to do, and I will do everything I can to create an environment which allows your natural mothering instincts to flourish. I will not interfere with it by putting pressure on you to go against your instincts. You're doing the most important job in the world, mothering our child." Avoid giving mixed messages such as, "I'll go along with you, but I feel you're making the baby too dependent." This serves only to create confusion in a new mother who is searching for her own parenting style and is already getting a lot of conflicting advice from outside the home.

## Settle down

Shortly before and after the birth of a baby, mothers have a nesting instinct. They like to prepare their house, their bedroom, for the arrival and care of the new baby. If at all possible, avoid major upheavals in your life such as changing jobs or moving during the first few months after baby arrives. Moving is the last thing new parents should be burdened with for at least six months after the baby arrives. To upset the nest is to upset the mother.

**The busy nest.** Bringing a new baby home often invites a whole rush of well-meaning friends and relatives who come to rally around the new parents and celebrate the homecoming. In my experience, nine times out of ten this winds up in disaster. The postpartum period should be a quiet nesting time in which the new family learns how to get along with each other in their new roles. No matter how well-meaning and "helpful," you usually wind up directing traffic and entertaining the bunch. New mothers usually have difficulty saying "no" to visitors. This should be a father's job. The father may need to stand guard at the front door and use some discretion in admitting visitors. Or you can simply hand out a sign: "Do not disturb. Mother and baby are resting and nesting." The wisest thing a friend can do is to send over the evening dinner with a note saying, "I'll see you all next week."

## Be sensitive

A new mother does not exercise wisdom in knowing when she is exceeding her ability to cope. She may try to persevere at all costs in her attempts to be the perfect mother. Be sensitive to the "I can't cope" red flags that indicate your wife may be approaching burnout. Father "tune-out" itself is a cause of mother burnout. Be prepared to step in and say, "I'll take over. You do something just for yourself."

There are certain times when a father take-over is particularly useful. One is during the night when your baby is fussing and not easily consoled; you are certain that he is not hungry and needs fathering more than food. Take your baby into another room and walk the floor until he drifts off to sleep, allowing mom to drift off to sleep, too. A bit of shift work is written into all contracts for nighttime parenting.

Another time for father take-over is in the late afternoon and early evening when baby has a fussy period just as you're coming home from work and wanting supper. Admittedly many fathers are tired from their long day's work, and the last thing they want is to be greeted by a tired mom and a fussy baby. This is the time, however, that some relief fathering is in order. Mother has been with the fussy baby all day long. Usually father is able to bring a fresh perspective to the situation, settle everyone down, and feel like a hero. This is the time for father to volunteer to take baby for a ride. Who says dads are not needed or wanted?

Another part of being a sensitive and caring father is to help your wife define her daytime priorities. Nighttime mothering becomes more difficult when mothers try to do too much during the day. Periodically take inventory of all those things which you could do, someone else could do, or that do not need to be done at all during those critical first few months. A simple statement such as "It doesn't bother me a bit that the house is messed up, because our baby is a baby for a very short time" conveys that you do not expect the house to be as neat as it was before the baby arrived. If you do expect that, then you take charge of getting it done without making your wife feel guilty about you doing "her" job. Ask her for specific ways you can help—laundry, vacuuming, scrubbing, or fixing a special meal. Find out what her sensitive spots are; for my wife it is a clean kitchen floor and a polished sink. Surprise her! It is easier to relax and enjoy mothering when your environment feels right.

### Delayed gratification
Avoid pressuring your wife into get-away weekends and holidays during the early stage of mother-infant attachment.

It is very common and very normal for a mother to feel that she does not want to leave her baby. If mother does feel that she needs a holiday, then support this by suggesting that you get away as a mother-father-child unit. Your wife will enjoy the freedom from household chores. Pressuring your wife into compromising her mothering instinct for her wifely duties usually results in a situation where everyone loses, including father. Realistic expectations for the growth and development of a new father include learning to accept a bit of delayed gratification.

Fathers, if you experience these normal "she's too attached" feelings, discuss them with your wife. Perhaps the two of you could read and discuss this chapter together. It is vitally necessary for husband and wife to share their ambivalent feelings with each other during the early months of parenting. Failure to work out these feelings usually results in a style of parenting which is not at all healthy: mother becomes more and more attached to her child, dad becomes more and more attached to his work, and both mom and dad drift farther and farther apart into an unending cycle of detachment. This is not healthy for mother, father, or baby.

### Fathering your baby to sleep

Mothers come equipped with the ultimate weapon for putting babies to sleep: the breast. This can leave fathers feeling helpless when it's time to put a fussy baby to sleep, and they may be tempted to hand baby off to mom. Yet there will be times when getting baby down for the night is dad's job, or when dad must care for a fussy baby in the middle of the night because mother desperately needs some sleep. Here are some ways that father can "nurse" a baby off to sleep.

**Be a warm fuzzy.** Tiny babies love to fall asleep on daddy's bare chest. Your warm skin plus the rhythm of your heartbeat and breathing movements will usually lull baby to sleep.

**Wearing down.** Put the baby in a baby sling or carrier and go for a walk. You can stroll around the house or take a walk around the neighborhood. You can even stand at your desk and sort bills and papers if you can keep swaying from side to side at the same time. The combination of the movement and being cuddled next to you will eventually lull baby to sleep. Keep strolling until baby is in a sound sleep, then go to the bed and slip the sling over your head as you gently lay baby down. If he stirs and awakens partially, you may have to walk some more or lie down next to him for a few minutes.

**Use your voice.** Father's low voice can be very soothing for a baby who needs to wind down to sleep. Sing something gentle and monotonous, or just talk to your baby in a quiet way. If you place his head against your chest near your neck, the vibrations

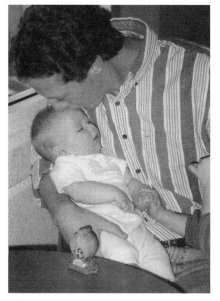

from your larynx will travel through your body to his and provide another soothing sensation.

**Bedtime rituals.** Be prepared for fathering-to-bed rituals, especially after your child is weaned. Because fathers usually have very little time with their children during the day, I feel that bedtime rituals should be primarily father's responsibility. Be prepared for your children to string these rituals out as long as they can. One father told me, "Our three-year-old just does not want to go to bed at night. When I finally do get him to wind down it takes me an hour to get him to settle down into bed." This father left for work in the morning before the child awakened and arrived home from work at six or seven in the evening. It is totally unrealistic to expect this child to go to bed at seven or eight o'clock. He hasn't been with his father all day. The child is simply demanding more prime together time in the evening.

A prolonged fathering-to-bed ritual is especially common

after a new baby comes along and undermines the older child's special place in the family. An older child will decide that since the tiny baby has so much of mommy's attention, "my time with dad right before bed is my special time and I'm going to have it!" This need for a special bedtime ritual reflects a need for more parenting. Children have a way of getting needs met during the evening that may not have been met during the day. Children need an uninterrupted one-on-one special time with dad.

## Bedtime Procrastination

*"It takes me at least an hour to put our three-year-old to bed. We have a large family, and we run out of time. I am an exhausted father."*

Procrastinating at bedtime is a common ploy of young children in a large family, especially following the arrival of a new baby. Sometimes the only time that a child gets one-on-one attention from his parents is at bedtime, and he is going to play this special time for all he can get. You can also expect this kind of behavior after you have been away for a while on a business trip. Bedtime is a receptive time for young children, and they are acutely aware of what you are saying or reading to them. Even though they may appear tired, they are more awake than you think. A three-year-old will catch you in the act if you try to hurry the ritual along a bit by skipping a page in a familiar story. Accept your child's desire for prime time with dad as a normal attachment phase, and be thankful that he wants to be with you.

I feel that bedtime rituals are primarily a father's responsibility. In most households, mothers usually get children up and get them going in the morning. It seems only fair that if mother winds the children up, father should wind them down. In a large family, do the best you can. One of the realities of fathering a large family is that you may not be able to give enough time to all your children all the time, and a certain amount of "group therapy" may be necessary in these bedtime rituals.

# When Dad's Away

Anticipate some sleep problems if dad is away for a few days. Nighttime restlessness is especially common when your child is accustomed to the family bed arrangement. Infants and children usually sense a change in family harmony with dad away and may be more restless at night. A mother shared this story with me: when father went away for one or two days, her two-year-old would point up at each airplane that flew over their house and say, "Airplane! Daddy home!" Dads really are missed.

# What's in It for You?

Dads, I want to share a thought with you from the bottom of my heart. One of the facts of married life is that a giving husband often gets back much more in return. Attachment fathering, during the day and at night, is one of the best long-term investments you're ever going to make. By being more involved you will know and enjoy your child more. This enjoyment will enhance your effectiveness as a father. Constantly give your wife and child the message, "I care for you." One of the greatest gifts you can give your child is to love his mother, and one of the greatest gifts you can give your wife is to be an involved father. Nighttime fathering is one of the greatest "I care" messages you can give both mother and child.

# Chapter 10

# Nighttime Parenting:
# the Key to Child Spacing

In developing countries, breastfeeding has long been considered an effective method of natural family planning. In Western cultures, however, breastfeeding has fallen into disrepute as a reliable contraceptive. Everyone seems to know a friend with two close-in-age children for whom it "didn't work."

Breastfeeding can be a reliable method of child spacing in ninety-five percent of mothers and may reach nearly one hundred percent reliability when coupled with other natural family planning methods, as long as the rules of the game are followed. Nighttime parenting plays an important role in suppressing a mother's fertility during her baby's first year.

## How Breastfeeding's Contraceptive Effect Works

The baby's sucking on the nipple stimulates the production of the mothering and milk-producing hormone, prolactin. The high level of circulating prolactin in the mother's blood suppresses the levels of estrogen and progesterone, the hormones which are necessary for ovulation and the preparation of the womb for implantation of a fertilized egg. When ovulation does not occur and there are no changes in the lining of the uterus, the mother does not have menstrual periods and is almost certainly infertile. The amount of sucking stimulation and the level of prolactin required to suppress these reproductive hormones vary from woman to woman, but in general, frequent and intense sucking stimulus, both day and night, is required to suppress ovulation.

As breastfeeding progresses and weaning approaches, the baby sucks less often and the mother's level of prolactin falls. Estrogen and progesterone levels rise and the first postpartum menstrual period occurs, a signal that the woman is or most likely soon will be fertile again. Shortly after this "warning menses," ovulation resumes and hence, fertility returns. In some mothers, particularly those whose babies are more than a year old, ovulation may occur without prior menstruation.

## Evidence for Breastfeeding's Contraceptive Effect

A review of scientific studies sheds some light on why this method of child spacing works for some women and doesn't appear to work for others. The suppression of ovulation and menstruation probably depends upon a consistently high level of prolactin in the mother's blood. Beginning supplemental feedings (either bottles or solid foods) has been shown to lower mothers' prolactin levels (Andersen and Schioler 1982). When artificial feedings were substituted for breastfeedings (rather than being used as an occasional complement to breastfeeding), mothers in this study showed a diminishing prolactin level. When supplemental feedings were introduced, babies also awakened less often at night. This also correlated with a decrease in the mothers' prolactin levels.

In another study, bottle-feeding mothers' prolactin returned to non-pregnant levels by four weeks postpartum (Howie 1982b). Breastfeeding mothers maintained a high prolactin level until weaning began. In those mothers who nursed an average of forty weeks, ovulation did not resume until 4.3 weeks after weaning.

Prolactin levels decline as the frequency of nursing decreases and the twenty-four-hour distribution of feedings becomes more concentrated during daylight hours.

An anthropologist has shown that the age at which children begin to sleep through the night is related to the return of menstruation (Knauer 1982). This study also suggests that even one extended period of separation from the child for twelve hours or more may trigger the return of menses. Other researchers found that fully lactating women who smoke more than fifteen cigarettes per day had suppressed prolactin levels and suggested that nicotine may block the sucking-induced rise in circulating prolactin (Howie 1982a).

Frequent breastfeeding is very important to maintaining high prolactin levels. Mothers who remained infertile the longest during lactation breastfed the longest, suckled their babies more frequently, maintained night feedings the longest, and introduced supplemental feedings the latest and most gradually (Howie 1982a). Ovulation returned in mothers when they breastfed fewer than six times per day and the total duration of sucking was less than sixty minutes a day.

Among mothers who conceived while still lactating, most conceived after weaning had begun (Howie and McNeilly 1982). Presumably the increasingly longer intervals between sucking episodes during the weaning process allowed the endocrine system to trigger ovulation. In another study of 500 mothers who were practicing full breastfeeding, only six mothers conceived while lactating but before weaning began (Giosia 1955). The researchers in this study concluded that breastfeeding is 99 percent effective as a method of contraception and that breastfeeding provided fertility protection for at least nine months as long as no substitute feedings were added. It has also been reported that the duration of lactational amenorrhea (absence of menstrual periods) tends to be longer in older than in younger women.

Women in developing countries where breastfeeding is a more effective method of child spacing show a more homogeneous breastfeeding pattern throughout a twenty-four-hour day (Jelliffe and Jelliffe 1978). Thirty-one percent of the baby's breastfeedings occur between 8:00 P.M. and 6:00 A.M. In contrast, Western mothers often try to bunch up the day feedings and space out night feedings in hopes of getting baby to "sleep through the night."

Studies on the ¡Kung tribe, a hunting and gathering people in Africa, have yielded some interesting information on natural mothering and natural family planning (Konner and Worthman 1980). In this culture, the infants are always in immediate physical proximity to the mother until two years of age or older. Separations are brief until age three-and-a-half when babies are often weaned because a new sibling is on the way. Babies sleep on the same skin mat with mother until weaned, and night nursing is the accepted norm. When questioned about night nursing, mothers responded that their infants nursed "many times" throughout the night without waking. The babies nursed in short, frequent bouts throughout the day, as often as several times per hour. Among these mothers of the ¡Kung tribe, the average birth interval was forty-four months. No other forms of contraception were used and there were no taboos on sexual intercourse during lactation.

A study of American women practicing natural mothering showed that similar child spacing results could be obtained in Western women who nursed their babies frequently (Elias 1984). Fifteen mothers who were members of La Leche League were compared with fifteen mothers who breastfed their babies in a more restricted fashion (standard care group). The results showed that La Leche League mothers had no menstrual periods for an average of 13.3 months. The standard group averaged 8.7 months of amenorrhea. LLL mothers nursed more frequently both day and night, and their babies weaned later. The researchers state that the most important factor associated with infertility during lactation was the duration of night nursing. The second most important factor was the age at which supplemental feedings were introduced.

Another study showing that American women can have long periods of lactation amenorrhea similar to women in underdeveloped countries was presented by Sheila Kippley (1974). In a group of twenty-nine women practicing natural mothering, there were no conceptions prior to the twelfth month postpartum, and the earliest conception without a warning menstrual period was at fifteen months. The mean duration of lactational amenorrhea was 14.6 months. The Kippleys listed the practices which most influenced the success of breastfeeding in prolonging lactation amenorrhea:

*No pacifiers used*

*No bottles used*

*No solids or liquids (other than breastfeeding)
for five months*

*No feeding schedules other than baby's*

*Presence of night feedings*

*Presence of lying-down feedings (naps, night nursing).*

## The Rules of the Game

Research on breastfeeding and fertility has led to the
development of the Lactational Amenorrhea Method of child
spacing, also known as LAM. This is being used by health
centers worldwide to help women recognize when their fertility
returns after childbirth. According to the LAM guidelines,
breastfeeding is an effective means of contraception as long as a
mother can answer "no" to the following questions:

1. *Have your menses returned?*

2. *Are you supplementing regularly or allowing long periods without breastfeeding, either during the day (more
   than four hours) or at night (more than six hours)?*

3. *Is your baby more than six months old?*

As long as a mother can answer "no" to all of these
questions, she has less than a two percent chance of becoming
pregnant.

The LAM guidelines are on the conservative side. Many
mothers will find that their breastfeeding style is effective as a
child-spacing method for much more than six months. Here are
the features of attachment parenting that help to prolong
postpartum infertility:

1. *Unrestricted breastfeeding without regard to daytime or
   nighttime scheduling.*

2. *Night nursing, preferably with mother and baby sleeping
   together.*

3. *Supplementary feedings delayed until at least six
   months. Solid foods should not substitute for breastfeeding but rather add to the baby's overall food intake.*

The return of menses following childbirth usually occurs before ovulation and serves as a warning that fertility may soon resume. In some lactating women, ovulation occurs before the first menses, and the mother may not know that her fertility has returned. Ovulation occurring before the first menses is more likely to happen after the baby is a year old or is beginning to wean. Most women's first menstrual periods while breastfeeding are anovulatory. In other words, most women do not ovulate and are not fertile until they have had at least one menstrual period.

Because the presence or absence of menstrual periods is not an infallible indication of fertility, it is wise for breastfeeding mothers to know about other signs of returning fertility. Women throughout history have learned to read their natural body processes to determine when they are fertile. Changes in the amount and type of cervical mucus are one of the signs that indicate imminent ovulation. Natural family-planning techniques are described in books listed at the end of this chapter. The best way to learn, especially while you're breastfeeding, is from a natural family planning instructor.

Natural mothering, especially the attachment style of nighttime parenting, can be a reliable method of child spacing. Parents who are blessed with a baby who sleeps through the night are also more likely to be blessed with another close-in-age child.

## References

Andersen, A. and Schioler, V. 1982. Influence of breastfeeding pattern on pituitary-ovarian axis of women in an industrialized community. *Am J Obstet Gynecol* 143:673.

Elias, M. F. et al. 1986. Nursing practices and lactation amenorrhoea. *J Biosoc Sci* 18:1-10.

Giosia, R. 1955. Incidence of pregnancy during lactation in 500 cases. *Am J Obstet Gynecol* 70:162.

Howie, P. W. and McNeilly, A. S. 1982. Effect of breastfeeding on human birth intervals. *J Reprod Fertil* 65:545.

Howie, P. W. et al. 1982a. Fertility after childbirth: Infant feeding patterns, basal PRL levels and postpartum ovulation. *Clin Endocrinol* 17:315.

Howie, P. W. et al. 1982b. Fertility after childbirth: Postpartum ovulation and menstruation in bottle and breastfeeding mothers. *Clin Endocrinol* 17:323.

Institute for Reproductive Health. *Guidelines: Breastfeeding Family Planning, and the Lactational Amenorrhea Method—LAM.* Washington, DC: Georgetown University, 1994.

Jelliffe, D. B. and Jelliffe, E. F. P. 1978. *Human Milk in the Modern World.* Oxford: Oxford University Press.

Kippley, J. F. and Kippley, S. K. 1984. *The Art of Natural Family Planning.* 3d ed. Cincinnati: Couple to Couple League.

Kippley, S. 1989. *Breastfeeding and Natural Child Spacing.* 2d ed. Cincinnati: Couple to Couple League.

Knauer, M. 1982. Postpartum fertility and breastfeeding. Paper presented at the 10th annual meeting of the Canadian Association for Physical Anthropologists, Guelph, Ontario.

Konner, M. and Worthman, C. 1980. Nursing frequency, gonadal function, and birth spacing among ¡Kung hunter-gatherers. *Science* 207:788.

Lewis, P. et al. 1991. The resumption of ovulation and menstruation in a well-nourished population of women breastfeeding for an extended period of time. *Fertil Steril* 55:529.

Winstein, M. *Your Fertility Signals: Using Them to Achieve or Avoid Pregnancy, Naturally.* 1994. St. Louis, MO: Smooth Stone Press.

# Chapter 11

# Common Disorders of Sleep and Arousal in Children

Nighttime is scary for little people. The strange activities which may occur during your child's sleep can put a strain on your nighttime parenting. These sleep disorders are classified into categories according to the states of sleep during which they occur.

## Disorders of REM Sleep

### *Nightmares*

The most common sleep disturbances in children between two and five years of age are nightmares. They occur during REM sleep. The term nightmare arises from the Teutonic word "mar," meaning devil. During the Middle Ages it was believed that nightmares were caused by a demon pressing upon the sleeper's chest.

Nightmares are often referred to as bad dreams, and that's exactly what they seem to be. Dreams in children are usually a reenactment of their previous daytime experiences, good or bad. Children are prone to distort reality in their nightmares; for example, a dog may appear as a monster. This distorted image easily awakens the child because it occurs during the REM or light state of sleep. The awakened child becomes even more terrified because he is not yet capable of distinguishing fantasies in dreams from reality. He believes "there really might be a monster in my room."

If your child insists there is a dragon in his room, play a little game with him: "Daddy went into your room and caught the dragon and put him in a cage." Don't be uneasy about fighting fantasy with fantasy. Another approach would be for dad to lie down with the child and parent him to sleep. Recurrent nightmares often lead to fear. The child becomes afraid to go to sleep for fear that another nightmare will appear. When a child becomes mature enough to understand the concept of dreaming and distinguish between fantasy and reality, effects of nightmares lessen.

**Minimize scary experiences during the day.** Children of three years of age can often relate the content of their dreams or nightmares. You may have to do a little detective work to find

out if there are any particular sources of disturbance in a child's day. Parents cannot completely eliminate nightmares in their children, but there are ways of lessening their terrifying effects. Try to minimize frightening daytime experiences which may reappear in your child's dreams. Television programs, scary books, music, and domestic strife can all affect your child's sleep. Pleasant parenting-to-bed rituals help a child enter sleep on a peaceful note. Scary prayers may induce scary dreams. The familiar rhyme "Now I Lay Me Down to Sleep" concludes with thoughts of death: "If I should die before I wake, I pray the Lord my soul to take." No child wants to enter sleep after the suggestion he might not awaken in the morning. Choose happier prayers and bedtime stories instead. (See Chapter Four for suggestions.)

**A secure awakening.** Provide a secure nighttime environment into which the frightened child can awaken. The terrified child who awakes alone does not have the immediate support he needs to help him distinguish fantasy from reality. Children who sleep with their parents (either in the parents' bed or bedroom) have fewer nightmares. Even children who sleep with siblings are known to have fewer nightmares (Anders and Weinstein 1972). Nighttime parenting helps minimize the effects of nightmares on attitudes toward sleep. If a child who is vulnerable to nightmares awakens into someone's caring arms, he is less likely to become afraid of going to bed.

## Disorders of Non-REM Sleep

Non-REM sleep disorders occur as the child is ascending from the deepest to the lightest stages of sleep. They include night terrors, sleepwalking, talking while sleeping, and bed-wetting. These disorders have several features in common:

*There is often a family history of similar sleep disorders.*

*These conditions usually occur in the first few hours after falling asleep.*

*They occur more frequently in males.*

*The child has no memory of the event and is very difficult to arouse during the event.*

*These disorders are most common between five and twelve years of age.*

In general the deeper the state of sleep the more strange and frightening the resulting activity. These disorders are thought to be caused by immaturity of the central nervous system. Most children completely outgrow these conditions, and they seldom imply any underlying psychological disturbance. Non-REM sleep disorders are not caused by a particular parenting style and are notoriously resistant to most forms of treatment.

### Night Terrors

The most frightening sleep disturbance for parents to witness is a case of night terrors. A child who has been previously in a state of deep sleep suddenly sits up in bed, lets out a piercing scream, and appears pale and terrified. He stares with eyes wide open at an imaginary object, cries incoherently, breathes heavily, perspires, and is completely unreceptive to his parents' attempts to console him. These attacks usually last from five to ten minutes. The child is not really awake and after the attack falls back into a deep calm sleep. Later he will not recall the experience. Although disturbing for parents, night terrors do not appear to bother the child because he is not fully awake when they occur, nor will he remember this bizarre nighttime activity. (In nightmares the child awakens, can remember the scary dream, and has difficulty reentering sleep without nighttime parenting.) Night terrors do not usually contribute to a fearful attitude toward sleep because the child does not remember them. Sleepwalking, talking, and bed-wetting may occur along with night terrors. These terrors lessen with age and maturity, and no medical treatment is needed.

### Sleepwalking

Most children experience at least one episode of sleepwalking. Many episodes may go unnoticed by parents. Sometimes the child may abruptly sit up with a wide-eyed vacant stare but not leave the bed. Some sleepwalkers have accompanying night terrors. When sleepwalking, the child appears clumsy, but surprisingly is coordinated enough to steer around obstacles without falling or injuring himself. Doors and drawers are often opened. The child's nighttime rounds may last from five to thirty minutes, and then he returns to bed without any recall of where he went or what he did. The sleepwalker is very difficult to arouse although about one-third of episodes do terminate with the child awakening.

Although sleepwalkers seldom hurt themselves, it's wise to create a safe environment in which your little sleeper can walk. You should eliminate hazardous objects from the sleeping wanderer's path: sharp-edged furniture, electrical cords, vaporizers, space heaters, etc. If your nocturnal navigator manages to get out of his own bedroom and awakens you, try to gently guide him back into his bed rather than attempting to awaken him fully. Talking may accompany sleepwalking. Speech during sleep can be surprisingly intelligible. The content of the talking is usually related to the experiences of the preceding day.

# Bed-Wetting

The age at which normal nighttime diaper-wetting becomes bed-wetting varies from family to family. In general, parents and children become increasingly concerned about this nocturnal nuisance around ages five or six years. By age three years the majority of children are dry at night and by age six, eighty-five percent of children enjoy nighttime dryness. Bed-wetting is nearly twice as common in boys as it is in girls. There is a hereditary component to bed-wetting. Children are more likely to have problems with bed-wetting if their parents were also bed-wetters.

## Bed-Wetting and Sleep

Bed-wetting may be considered a sleep problem, or more accurately, a disorder of arousal. The child sleeps too deeply to recognize that he needs to empty his bladder. Observant parents have figured this out for themselves: "He sleeps so deeply, he doesn't even know he's wetting the bed." These deep sleepers are not aware of their bladder sensation at night, much less are they able to control it. Some bed-wetters have different sleep cycles than children who are dry at night. Bed-wetting children descend into deep sleep quickly and remain in the state of deep sleep longer. The first bed-wetting episode of the night occurs near the end of this prolonged period of deep sleep just before the first REM period, one to three hours after the child falls asleep. This sequence explains why many children awaken as they enter the first REM period to find themselves already wet.

In some children, bed-wetting may also be related to differences in the hormonal control of urination. Some bed-wetters may have a deficiency of ADH (anti-diuretic hormone), the hormone that is released during sleep to concentrate the urine so that the kidneys produce a smaller volume and the bladder doesn't get too full. Bed-wetters may produce a lot of urine while sleeping, but are just not aware that they need to empty their bladders. In addition, a small number of children have small bladders that are more easily overfilled.

### Myths about Bed-Wetting

Bed-wetting is not a psychological problem. It does not mean that your child is too lazy to get up, is using bed-wetting as a control issue, or is manipulating the family. Misunderstandings about bed-wetting have kept it from being viewed as a legitimate medical problem. If the lungs malfunction, the child is treated for asthma, and gets a lot of sympathy. If the bladder malfunctions, the child is thought to be lazy, stubborn, and immature. It's a myth that children don't care. Really, what child would want to wake up in a wet, smelly bed every morning for years, and start each morning by stripping the bed and carrying wet sheets to the washer?

### A Nine-Step Approach to Achieving Dry Nights

Here's the step-by-step approach to bed-wetting that I have developed during my twenty-five years in pediatric practice. I have found that this time-tested approach works in at least seventy percent of children.

**Step one: Keep a diary.** What is different about the days that precede a dry night in comparison to the days that lead to a wet night? Is there a relationship between the bed-wetting and certain foods, drinks, life events, family events, school situations, daytime bowel and bladder patterns, or family dynamics? Food allergies, carbonated and/or caffeinated beverages, problems with constipation, or life stress may all affect the ability to stay dry at night. However, most parents are not able to pinpoint a specific environmental cause.

**Step two: Have your doctor evaluate the situation.** Sometimes bed-wetting can be attributed to a specific medical problem. You should eliminate this possibility before moving on to a night training program.

**Step three: Explain the problem to your child.** In order to achieve success, your child must cooperate with the program and take some responsibility for his nighttime dryness. Achieving nighttime dryness calls for a team approach, but ultimately, it's the child's bladder and the child who has to learn what to do.

Here's how I explain bed-wetting to six-year-olds: "Your bladder is like a balloon the size of a baseball. Tiny nerves inside the balloon tell your brain when your bladder is full and you need to go to the bathroom to empty it. There is a big donut muscle at the end of your bladder that squeezes down and keeps your pee inside until you get to the toilet. If you can't go to the bathroom right away, the muscle helps you hold on to the pee until you can go. But at night your brain is asleep, and when the bladder says, 'I'm too full, I've got to go,' the brain says, 'Don't bother me, I'm sleeping.' So the pee comes out on the sheets instead of in the toilet."

After you've helped your child understand what's going on in his body when he wets the bed, explain that you're going to work with him to help his bladder and his brain listen to each other at night so that he can wake up and go to the bathroom.

**Step four: Improve bladder-emptying.** Just before your child goes to bed, take him to the bathroom and encourage him to "go three times" or "grunt, grunt, grunt" while urinating, to squeeze out all the pee. Many children, tired and in a hurry, go to bed with a half-full bladder.

**Step five: Wake your child at night to urinate.** Most children wet their bed within a few hours after falling asleep, and most parents go to bed a few hours after their children do. So just before you retire, wake your child and take him to the bathroom. Carrying a sleeping child to the bathroom isn't going to accomplish a complete bladder emptying. He has to be awake enough to sense what is going on in his bladder, so make him walk to the bathroom. When you get there, have him splash water on his face or use a cool wash rag to wake himself up, and then go through the "grunt three times to push the pee out" routine. If your child still wets his bed despite waking him up when you go to bed, set your alarm and wake him again two to three hours later. Once your child has a few dry nights, he will become more motivated to cooperate with these drills. Some children may even be able to respond to an alarm clock on their own, and get up and go to the bathroom without waking their parents.

**Step six: Do bladder-training drills.** Just before your child goes to bed or when he goes back to bed after being awakened to use the bathroom, talk him through the process of getting up to pee at night. "I'm going to feel my bladder get big and then I will get up and go to the bathroom. I will splash water on my face and grunt, grunt, grunt to push the pee out." Have some fun with these conversations, so that your child has positive feelings about getting control of his body.

**Step seven: Do bladder conditioning exercises during the day.** These increase bladder capacity, neuromuscular control, and awareness of bladder fullness during the day which may carry over into the night. Try these exercises:

1. *Progressive urine withholding. Encourage your child to drink large amounts of fluid and voluntarily hold his urine for increasingly longer times, even though he has the urge to void. As your child's bladder capacity increases, like a stretched balloon, it should be able to hold more without having to empty so often.*

2. *Stop and go. Advise your child to start and stop his stream many times during urination. This gives a child*

*the awareness that he can actually control his bladder if he wants to. Check with your doctor before trying these exercises. They may not be suitable for some children, especially girls with a history of urinary tract infections.*

**Step eight: Try a bladder-conditioning device.** These devices consist of a moisture-sensitive pad that the child wears inside his underwear. When one or two drops of urine strike the pad, a buzzer or vibrator awakens the child so that he can complete his urination in the toilet. I have used these devices for twenty years in pediatric practice, and my experience is that they are effective around seventy to eighty percent of the time if they are used along with the drills described above. These devices work using the principle of conditioned response. The child subconsciously learns to associate the alarm with the feeling of having a full bladder. Eventually he learns to "beat the buzzer" and gets up and goes to the bathroom when his bladder is full, even before the alarm sounds.

Before using the alarm system at night, have several practice sessions. With your child lying in bed, set off the alarm and then walk with your child to the bathroom, where he will wake himself up by splashing water on his face and then empty his bladder.

It may take several weeks for the number of dry nights to increase. Relapses are common after a few months, so you may need to go through another round of using the device and the drills. Parents sometimes report that the alarm they ordered out of a catalogue didn't work. That's because they didn't do the drills, which are a vital part of the whole bladder-conditioning package.

**Step nine: Positive reinforcement.** Reward your child for working on his bed-wetting problem. Use a chart with stickers or D for dry and W for wet nights. After an agreed-upon number of D's, he gets a reward, perhaps a special outing with you. Soon the feeling of mastery over his bladder becomes its own reward.

### Drugs for Dry Nights

Drugs do not cure bed-wetting, they simply control it until the child matures out of it. Your doctor may suggest DDAVP (desmopressin), which diminishes the production of urine at night, similar to the natural action of the child's own anti-diuretic hormone. This medicine comes in a tablet or nasal spray, which your child uses before bedtime for two or three months, and then gradually discontinues. Many children have a relapse and need another course of the medication. DDAVP works for 80 to 90 percent of children who don't respond to other treatments. DDAVP is safe, effective, and has minimal side-effects, but it is expensive.

One of the oldest medications for bed-wetting, and one which I personally do not recommend, is imipramine (Tofranil), which is basically an antidepressant. It has side-effects such as blood pressure changes, irregular heartbeat, anxiety, insomnia, dry mouth, blurred vision, nausea, vomiting, diarrhea, dizziness, drowsiness, and headaches. Also, bed-wetting often resumes when the treatment stops. Overdose can cause convulsions. With the nine-step approach the use of this drug is rarely necessary.

## Nighttime Thumb-Sucking

Some children cannot drift off to sleep without the comfort of their thumbs, and some children suck their thumbs habitually during most of the night. The majority of children suffer no ill effects from nighttime thumb-sucking, but the occasional child may put enough pressure on his upper front teeth to cause an overbite and need orthodontic repair.

There has been a lot of speculation and controversy as to why some children persist in the habit of nighttime thumbsucking. In 1977 two Turkish researchers studied fifty children between ages one and seven who were habitual thumb-suckers (Ozturk and Ozturk). These researchers compared children who sucked their thumbs with those who did not. The study showed that thumb-suckers tended to be bottle-fed rather than breastfed. The later the child was weaned the less likely he was to suck his thumb. The thumbsucking children tended to have been fed on a schedule rather than on demand. Most significant was the finding that ninety-six percent of thumb-suckers had been left to fall asleep alone after having been fed. Among the children who did not suck their thumbs there was not a single child who was left alone to fall asleep. Instead these children were given the opportunity to suck until they fell asleep.

These researchers suggested that sleep is a regressive activity during which there is a return to more primitive reflexes such as sucking and hand-to-mouth actions. While falling asleep the child's primitive sucking reflex is stimulated and the sucking drive is intensified. The researchers theorized that if the infant goes to sleep while sucking at the breast, bottle, or pacifier, the sucking drive will be satisfied and the hand-to-mouth reflex will not stimulate sucking later in the evening. In other words, a need filled in early infancy disappears; a need which is not filled does not go away but reappears, sometimes as an undesirable habit. In my own practice I have noticed that babies who are nursed down to sleep, offered unrestricted night nursings, and not weaned until they are ready are much less likely to become habitual thumb-suckers.

### References

Anders, T. F. and Weinstein, P. 1972. Sleep and its disorders in infants and children: A review. *Pediatrics* 50:312.

Broughton, B. 1968. Sleep disorders: Disorders of arousal. *Science* 159:1070.

Campbell, K. 1981. Association of the domestic set-up with sleeping difficulties in children under three years of age. *Med J Aust* 2:254.

Ozturk, M. and Ozturk, O. M. 1977. Thumbsucking and falling asleep. *Bri J Med Psychol* 50:95.

# Chapter 12

# Nighttime Parenting and Sudden Infant Death Syndrome

Sudden infant death syndrome (SIDS), also known as crib death, is one of the most tragic of all nighttime crises. A healthy infant is put to bed and is later found dead for no apparent reason. Parents are devastated, left wondering why, and while medical research has produced a number of theories about SIDS, it still cannot explain exactly what happens when an infant dies unexpectedly during sleep.

SIDS is the leading cause of death of infants between one month and one year of age. It strikes infants most often between one and six months of age with the peak incidence around three months. It happens more often in the winter months and usually occurs between 10:00 P.M. and 10:00 A.M. Certain environmental factors may increase the risk of SIDS. It occurs more frequently in families from lower socioeconomic groups. It is also more frequent if mothers are smokers or drug abusers. SIDS is not caused by overlaying the baby or by choking.

While there is evidence that the occurrence of SIDS has declined in recent years, new parents often worry a great deal about their baby dying unexpectedly from SIDS. For many years, doctors could do little to alleviate these fears, because medical science believed that little could be done to prevent SIDS deaths. Newer studies, however, suggest that various factors that are under parents' control influence SIDS risk. While you cannot guarantee that your baby will not become a SIDS victim, you can lessen the chances. I have come to believe that practicing the attachment style of nighttime parenting is one of the most important things you as a parent can do to lower the risk of SIDS in your baby.

## SIDS and Sleep

Because the infant dies during sleep, SIDS can be thought of as a sleep disorder. The infant who becomes a SIDS victim may be unable to control his breathing automatically during sleep or to arouse from sleep in response to a breathing problem. In order to understand this theory of SIDS causation it is first necessary to understand how the infant normally continues breathing while sleeping.

### Automatic Breathing Mechanisms
The purpose of breathing is to take in life-sustaining oxygen and expel carbon dioxide, a waste product. In order for the body to function there must be a balance of just the right amount of oxygen and carbon dioxide in the blood. If the oxygen is too low or the carbon dioxide too high, the body will not function properly. In order to maintain this balance, tiny sensor cells called chemoreceptors are located along some major blood vessels. These sensors detect changes in oxygen and carbon dioxide. If the oxygen gets too low or the carbon dioxide too high, the chemoreceptors send messages to the brain to speed up breathing. During waking hours breathing is regulated by voluntary mechanisms in the nervous system in addition to these chemoreceptors. During sleep, the body is particularly dependent on these chemoreceptors to keep breathing going. As the sleeper descends through the various levels of sleep and diminished consciousness, breathing slows, and these automatic mechanisms become more important.

In the first few months, the infant's automatic breathing mechanisms are immature. When watching a sleeping baby breathe, you will notice that his breathing lacks a regular pattern. Periodically he appears to stop breathing, sometimes for as long as ten to fifteen seconds, and then self-starts without any apparent problem. This is called periodic breathing and is normal for the tiny infant. The younger or the more premature the baby, the more irregular the breathing pattern and the more noticeable the periodic breathing. As the baby matures (around six months), breathing patterns during sleep become more regular and periodic breathing lessens. The episodes when the baby stops breathing are called **apnea**. Sometimes they are prolonged for more than fifteen to twenty seconds, and the heart rate drops significantly (greater than twenty percent). As a response to this sleep apnea, either the automatic start mechanisms click on or the infant awakens. Either way, normal breathing resumes.

Sometimes the apnea is prolonged, and breathing fails to start again. When this happens, infants who are hooked up to apnea monitors show signs that the oxygen in the blood is at a dangerously low level: the heart rate becomes alarmingly slow, and the infant turns pale, blue, and limp. An observer must intervene and arouse the infant. Sometimes a simple touch will trigger the self-starting mechanism; sometimes the infant must be aroused from sleep in order to breathe; sometimes mouth-to-mouth resuscitation is necessary to initiate breathing again. Infants who have experienced an apnea episode that required outside intervention to restart their breathing are called near-miss SIDS. In other words, they would have died had someone not intervened. Tragically, some infants stop breathing permanently, succumbing to SIDS.

### SIDS as a Sleep Disorder

It is plausible that in some cases SIDS is a basic sleep disorder. Normal infants have a protective mechanism which helps them awaken easily in response to apnea. For unknown reasons, an infant who becomes a SIDS victim or has a near-miss SIDS episode does not have the ability to arouse easily from sleep in response to a life-threatening breathing problem.

The study of SIDS is hampered by the fact that researchers can draw very little information from the infants who die. Most of the current information about the causes of SIDS has been learned from other sources. Scientists have studied high-risk infants who subsequently succumb to SIDS, as well as infants who have near-miss SIDS episodes and siblings of SIDS victims who presumably may show a tendency toward breathing problems that could lead to SIDS.

**Impaired arousal responses.** The peak incidence of SIDS is around three months, which coincides with the time most babies begin to sleep "better," that is, to spend a larger percentage of sleep time in quiet sleep. During quiet sleep, infants are less responsive to the breathing-stimulating effects of low oxygen and increased carbon dioxide (Harper 1982).

Studies of near-miss infants and siblings of SIDS infants show that these babies have fewer night-waking episodes. In the first few months, infants normally have frequent periods of night-waking as they ascend from quiet sleep to active sleep and back into quiet sleep. Researchers have suggested that arousal from sleep may be essential for resumption of breathing in babies who have less effective self-starting mechanisms (Harper 1981). High risk infants (that is, siblings of SIDS victims and near-miss SIDS cases) show fewer night-waking episodes during the transition from quiet sleep to active sleep. Difficulty with waking up may place infants at higher risk for SIDS.

**Impaired chemoreceptor sensitivity.** High risk infants show a higher heart rate during quiet sleep (Leistner 1980). The heart rate increases to compensate for a lowered oxygen level. This suggests that high risk infants have chronically low oxygen levels during quiet sleep. Post-mortem examinations of SIDS victims reveal tissue changes that reflect the effects of chronic hypoxia (low oxygen).

In one study high risk infants showed a diminished arousal response to lowered oxygen or increased carbon dioxide during chemoreceptor challenge tests (McCulloch 1982). When the carbon dioxide in their environment increased, high risk infants took longer to awaken, as shown by eye opening and crying, and required a higher carbon dioxide level to stimulate breathing. The high risk infants were less likely to awaken as the oxygen levels in their blood decreased. They also required a lower level of oxygen to initiate awakening than did infants at low risk for SIDS. The researchers' interpretation of this data suggests that SIDS victims show deficient arousal responses to sleep apnea.

High risk infants also show more frequent episodes of sleep apnea and periodic breathing (Guillemmault 1981). This apnea occurs most frequently between 1:00 A.M. and 6:00 A.M. and within ten minutes of awakening. The infants who woke most often at night had fewer episodes of apnea.

In summary, these findings suggest that high risk infants have two breathing abnormalities:

1. *Impaired chemoreceptor sensitivity, that is, they don't breathe when they need to.*

2. *Impaired arousal response in the nervous system to a breathing problem.*

In other words, high risk infants don't awaken when their breathing stops.

**Active sleep guards against SIDS.** Sleep studies have shown that the onset of active sleep (REM sleep) stimulates breathing and heart rate. On the basis of their studies, researchers hypothesized that:

> Active sleep "protects" human infants from SIDS. The predominance and tenacity of the active sleep state in the newborn period accounts for the paradoxical immunities to SIDS in the first month of life. The peak risk period for SIDS coincides with the rapid decrease in active sleep between two and three months of age. By six months of age, cardiopulmonary compensatory mechanisms in quiet sleep are more mature and the risk of death (from failure of these mechanisms) is reduced (Baker and McGinty 1977).

In other words, infants are not designed to sleep through the night until they're mature enough to do so safely.

## Infant Temperament, Sleep, and SIDS
Studies suggesting that SIDS is more common among babies with so-called easier temperaments provide further evidence

that SIDS is a disorder of arousal. In one study, researchers interviewed parents about behavioral patterns of forty infants who were victims of SIDS. The SIDS infants had tended to be less active and reacted less intensely to stimuli. In other words, they were "easy" babies (Naeye 1976).

Another study, however, failed to show any difference in temperament between normal infants and near-miss SIDS infants and siblings of SIDS infants (Weissbluth 1982). However, within the group of near-miss SIDS, infants who showed low activity and low intensity on temperament scores also showed more apnea and periodic breathing during sleep. Also, the near-miss SIDS infants who were rated as less sensitive to external stimuli when awake had more apnea episodes during sleep. But the authors cautioned against concluding that all less sensitive infants are necessarily at increased risk for SIDS.

Infant temperament studies have shown that less sensitive infants have fewer episodes of night-waking (Carey 1974). In colicky infants, SIDS is thought to be uncommon as long as the colic persists. Although the relationship between infant temperament and SIDS remains unclear, it is possible that SIDS is a disorder of sensitivity to arousal stimuli. In an infant who already has other SIDS risk factors, a more sensitive temperament may lower the risk of SIDS.

### SIDS and Breastfeeding

For many years, SIDS researchers maintained that there was no difference in the incidence of SIDS between breastfed and artificially fed babies, but newer studies have shown that infants who were never breastfed may have two to three times the risk of dying of SIDS. Breastfeeding's protective effect has been confirmed by research in New Zealand (Mitchell 1991), England (Fleming 1994), and the United States (Hoffman 1988). There are a number of possible explanations for the lowered risk of SIDS in breastfed babies. Breastfeeding protects infants from respiratory and gastrointestinal infections, and these have been shown to contribute to SIDS risk. Human milk enhances the development of the central nervous system, providing vital nutrients for the process of myelination, the development of an insulating sheath around nerves. Better brains may provide babies with better respiratory control during sleep. Breastfed babies sleep less soundly than artificially fed infants and are more likely to sleep with their mothers; thus, they may be more easily aroused when they experience a stop-breathing episode. While SIDS does occur in breastfed babies, breastfeeding is one way of lowering the risk.

### SIDS and Mothering Skills

While inadequate mothering is certainly not the cause of SIDS, it may be a contributing factor in those infants already at risk. Studies have shown a much higher incidence of SIDS among infants of less committed and less skilled mothers. An interesting study in Sheffield, England showed that improving mothering skills can decrease the risk of SIDS (Carpenter and Emory 1977). Researchers selected a group of high risk infants from a total of 15,000 babies. They divided these high risk babies into two groups: one group received extra postnatal follow-up exams and biweekly home visits by a public health nurse. The mothers in this special attention group also received education in mothering skills, nutrition, hygiene, and recognizing when their infants were sick. The second group received no special attention. The rate of SIDS was three times greater in the group who received no special attention, 10.6 per thousand compared to 3.2 per thousand in the special attention group.

# How Parenting Style Can Decrease the Risk of SIDS

What are the practical implications of this research for nighttime parenting? In the 1984 edition of this book I proposed the following hypothesis:

> *In those infants at risk for SIDS, natural mothering (unrestricted breastfeeding and sharing sleep with baby) will lower the risk of SIDS.*

This was a new idea at the time, one that I based upon my reading of SIDS research and my understanding of the close relationship between a breastfeeding mother and her baby. My hope was that publication of this hypothesis would stimulate more scientific research in this area. Fifteen years later, in 1999, I am happy to report that the body of evidence available to support my original idea is growing, and experts are beginning to understand how a mother's presence with her baby during sleep can help to prevent SIDS. Here's the reasoning behind my theory—and the evidence and ideas that support it.

### Sharing Sleep May Lower SIDS Risk

If SIDS is related to a diminished arousal response during sleep in some infants, it follows that anything which increases the infant's sensitivity or the mother's awareness of her baby may decrease the risk of SIDS. This is exactly what sharing sleep and night nursing do.

**Shared sleep cycles.** As a father of several all-night nursers, I have noticed that mother and baby often stir or awaken briefly at the same time. The nursing pair have a heightened awareness of each other. A study of mothers and babies co-sleeping in a sleep laboratory has documented the shared awakenings of co-sleeping breastfeeding mothers and babies (McKenna 1994). When one stirred, coughed, moved, or changed positions, so did the other. The researchers also demonstrated that co-sleeping mother and babies were often in the same stage of sleep during the night. Clearly, the presence of each affects the other.

Anthropological studies have shown that the rate of SIDS is approximately three to four times higher in cultures where mothers do not sleep with their babies. For example, the SIDS rate seems to be high in Native American cultures where babies sleep on cradle boards. More extensive research is needed on exactly what happens when mother and baby sleep close to each other. It seems odd that science demands proof that co-sleeping is good for babies, since mother and babies sharing sleep has been the norm through most of human history, but there is still much to learn about how mothers help their babies develop. Meanwhile, I have to ask, if there were fewer cribs, would there be fewer crib deaths?

**Breathing Harmony**

Baby has become accustomed to mother's breathing rhythm in utero. After birth, mother continues to act as a respiratory pacemaker reminding baby to breathe.

**Immunological Protection**

Infants who share sleep nurse more often. Breast milk provides extra protection from three to six months of age when baby's own immunity is lowest and the risk of SIDS is highest.

**Mutual Awareness**

Breastfeeding mothers and babies who share sleep have more REM and less non-REM sleep. Sensitivity to each other is increased in REM sleep: blood oxygen and sensitivity to breathing stimuli are diminished in non-REM sleep.

**Hormones Increased**

Breastfeeding especially at night stimulates the release of prolactin, the relaxing hormone which makes it easier for a mother to be responsive to her baby's cues.

**Back Sleeping**

Babies who sleep next to their mothers tend to sleep on their back or their side, especially after coming off the breast.

**Touching**

The skin is rich in nerves and touching acts as a respiratory stimulant. Tactile stimulation is enhanced when baby is breastfeeding and held close to mother's breathing, moving body.

**Sucking at Night**

Infants who share sleep with their mothers suck more, and babies show REM sleep patterns during sucking. Sucking improves the amount of oxygen in the blood of premature infants.

**Enhances Development**

Babies who have more nursing and touching time with their mothers show enhanced overall development: this may carry over into enhanced cardiorespiratory and neurologic development.

*How sharing sleep protects against SIDS.*

**Babies breathe better when sharing sleep.** My interest in the relationship between shared sleep and lowered risk of SIDS led me to gather some data on our youngest daughter, Lauren, when she was eight weeks old. Using sophisticated monitoring equipment in our home, a technician and I monitored Lauren's sleep on two separate nights. On one night, my wife, Martha, slept beside Lauren. On the other night, Martha nursed Lauren to sleep in our bed, but slept in an adjacent room. We found that Lauren's heart rate and her breathing were more regular during shared sleep, with far fewer low points in blood oxygen levels. Monitoring another mother-infant pair produced similar results.

Obviously, this was a very small sample group, from which it is impossible to draw statistically valid conclusions. However, our data suggest a theory that needs further testing: a baby who sleeps next to mother is likely to experience fewer apnea episodes and thus may be at lower risk for SIDS. While again, this is not scientifically tested evidence, I have had many breastfeeding and co-sleeping mothers in my practice tell me that they felt their own breathing helped their babies continue to breathe. They have noticed that their infants breathe more rhythmically lying next to mother in bed than they do in a crib. One mother, whose baby was monitored with an apnea monitor during sleep because of breathing difficulties, found that the alarm went off frequently when the baby slept alone, but not at all when the baby slept with mother.

**Babies are not designed to sleep through the night.** If SIDS is related to a baby's inability to arouse himself from sleep, it follows that babies are simply not designed to sleep through the night, not until they are mature enough to avoid respiratory failure during quiet sleep. Parents need to be aware that studies that show that babies sleep through the night at a given age were performed in artificial settings: a sleep laboratory, a hospital, or some other nighttime environment in which baby sleeps alone. Sleeping alone is considered the norm, so babies are studied sleeping alone in cribs. The conclusions drawn from these studies of "normal" sleeping infants are that infants begin to have a higher proportion of quiet or non-REM sleep and sleep in longer stretches ("through the night") by three months of age—incidentally, the peak age for SIDS. From erroneously set-up experiments come erroneous norms. Parents (and doctors) should not use these norms as a justification for training babies to sleep through the night at a given age.

One study suggests that the sleep norms extracted from these older studies (that babies sleep through the night by six months of age) may be attributed to the early weaning and separate sleeping practices of Western culture (Elias 1986). Researchers compared sleep/wake patterns in infants reared with two different parenting styles. One group consisted of sixteen mother-infant pairs, called the standard care group, who breastfed but tended to wean earlier and sleep separately. The other was made up of sixteen mother-infant pairs from La Leche League. These pairs breastfed more frequently throughout the day, weaned later, and usually slept together. Sleep/wake patterns developed differently in the two groups of infants. The sleep periods of the infants in the standard care group increased in duration from a median of 6.5 hours at two months to 8 hours at four months of age. The sleep periods of infants in the La Leche League group never increased from the median of four hours; they continued to awaken at night throughout the period of study.

These researchers also showed that the combination of nursing and sharing sleep had the greatest effect on sleep patterns. Babies who nursed and shared sleep with their mothers slept shorter stretches at a time; those who nursed but did not share sleep slept longer; and babies who neither nursed nor shared sleep slept the longest.

The human infant is meant to be a continuous contact species. The composition of milk of each species gives a clue to the infant care practices natural to that species. Animals who leave their young for extended periods produce a milk high in fat and protein which satisfies the young for a relatively long period of time between feedings. Human milk is relatively low in fat and protein, necessitating frequent, seemingly continuous, nursing. The human infant is meant to be carried in arms during the day and nestled with mother in bed at night—not trained into a separate sleeping arrangement before he is ready.

### SIDS and Illness

Attachment parenting may also lower the risk of SIDS by keeping babies healthier. Approximately two-thirds of SIDS infants have a respiratory or intestinal illness within a few days before death. It is thought that an infection in the breathing passages (stuffy nose or cold) may contribute to narrowing of the airways in an infant already at risk of SIDS. Colds and other illnesses may contribute to SIDS by disrupting baby's sleep. Sleep fragmentation and deprivation hinder the arousal responses to respiratory stimuli (Keens and Van der Hol 1984). Breastfed infants have fewer colds and intestinal illnesses in the first year. Mothers who share sleep with their babies are more aware of their babies' needs and are more available to help them handle colds. This is another way in which nursing and sharing sleep may lower the risk of SIDS.

### Sharing Sleep Develops Intuitive Mothers

Mothers who respond to their babies' cries and who nurse and share sleep with their babies seem to know their babies better and develop more intuitive mothering skills. Studies have shown that improving the mother's intuitive skills may lower the risk of SIDS (Carpenter and Emory 1974). This may be another way in which attachment nighttime parenting lowers the risk of SIDS.

## Other Nighttime Parenting Practices That May Lower the Risk of SIDS

In the last ten years, the medical community has begun to educate parents on what they can do to lower their baby's risk of SIDS. The recommendations are based on studies of large groups of infants that have compared babies who became SIDS victims with babies who did not. The findings of these studies can help you give your baby a safe sleeping environment.

### Back to Sleep

The recommendation that babies be put down on their backs to sleep has been the most publicized feature of public health campaigns on SIDS risk-reduction, and SIDS rates have fallen dramatically in countries that have implemented public information programs on SIDS. Research has shown a correlation between prone (stomach-down) sleeping and SIDS, and cultures in which infants are traditionally put down on their backs to sleep have lower SIDS rates. Therefore pediatricians have begun to tell parents to place their babies on their backs when putting them down to sleep, at least until about six months of age.

Why the connection between back-sleeping and lower SIDS rates? It may be that babies who sleep in the prone position sleep more soundly and have more difficulty rousing from sleep when their breathing is compromised. With their faces snuggled into the mattress, they may be more likely to breathe their own exhaled air, which contains less oxygen and more carbon dioxide than the room air. Re-breathing is more likely to occur when baby is sleeping tummy-down on a soft surface, his face sunk into pillows, the bed clothes, or the mattress. This is why babies should not use pillows and why they should sleep only on a firm mattress.

Sharing sleep may actually help to promote back or side-sleeping. Babies who sleep with their mothers tend to end up on their backs or sides as they come off the breast. Back-sleeping also gives them easier access to the breast throughout the night. Mothers and babies who sleep together seem to enjoy facing each other as they sleep. (For more information on infant sleep positions, see Chapter Four.)

### *Avoid Overheating*

Research has also found an association between overheating and SIDS. Overheating may cause respiratory control centers in some infants to fail. The association with overheating may also help to explain why SIDS rates are higher in the winter months, when parents take more care to be sure a baby is warm enough. A little bit of overheating is not the concern here, but rather too much clothing and too much bedding in a room that itself may be too warm.

When you dress your baby for sleep, consider how much clothing or how many blankets you yourself would need to be comfortable. Most full-term babies need no more layers than adults. If the back of your baby's neck feels warm or sweaty, remove a layer of clothing. A baby sleeping with parents may need less clothing than a baby sleeping alone, since adult bodies provide added warmth. Don't bundle up a baby who has a fever; this only makes a hot body hotter. And don't cover a baby's head while sleeping. An hours-old newborn may benefit from this heat-conserving practice, but it can lead to overheating in babies more than a few days old.

### Give Your Baby a Safe Sleeping Environment

Researchers are uncertain what role suffocation plays in SIDS, but some infants who have died of SIDS have been found with bedding over their mouths or noses. Some SIDS cases may actually be the result of overlaying—an adult or older child rolling on top of the baby, preventing the baby from breathing. See Chapter Three for information on safety while sharing sleep and Chapter Fourteen for tips on crib safety and safe bedding.

### Don't Smoke

Many studies have shown a correlation between SIDS and parental smoking. Smoking during pregnancy affects fetal development and increases the risk of prematurity and low birthweight as well as SIDS. Exposure to cigarette smoke after birth also increases SIDS risk which is why fathers as well as mothers should not smoke. Toxins from cigarette smoke can affect a baby's heart rate and breathing. Children of parents who smoke have more respiratory infections, which may be another reason that smoking is associated with an increased risk of SIDS. There are many compelling reasons to quit smoking when you enter parenthood, and the increased risk of SIDS tops the list.

## A Final Word

If you are interested in learning more about SIDS, you may want to read my book *SIDS: A Parent's Guide to Understanding and Preventing Sudden Infant Death Syndrome*. It contains more detailed information about SIDS research and what parents can do to lower their baby's risk. It also contains information for grieving parents who have lost a child to SIDS. While I believe that there is much parents can do to lower the risk of SIDS in their infant, I do not mean to suggest that parents of a baby who dies of SIDS are in any way at fault. SIDS is a terrible tragedy, and it is not entirely preventable.

## References

Baker, T. L. and McGinty, D. J. 1977. Reversal of cardiopulmonary failure during active sleep in hypoxic kittens: Implications for sudden infant death. *Science* 198:419.

Carey, W. B. 1974. Night-waking and temperament in infancy. *J Pediatr* 84:756.

Carpenter, R. G. and Emory, J. L. 1977. Final results of study of infants at risk of sudden infant death. *Nature* 268:724.

Elias, M. F. 1986. Sleep-wake patterns of breastfed infants in the first two years of life. *Pediatrics* 77:322-39.

Fleming, P. J. 1994. *Proceedings of the Fourth Annual SIDS Alliance National Conference.* Orlando, November 9-12.

Guillemmault, C. et al. 1981. Sleep parameters and respiratory variables in near-miss sudden infant death syndrome infants. *Pediatrics* 68:354.

Guntheroth, W. 1982. *Crib Death.* Mount Kisco, NY: Futura Publishing.

Harper, R. M. et al. 1981. Periodicity of sleep states is altered in infants at risk for the sudden infant death syndrome. *Science* 213:1030.

Harper, R. M. et al. 1982. Developmental patterns of heart rate and heart rate variability during sleep and waking in normal infants and infants at risk for the sudden infant death syndrome. *Sleep* 5:28.

Hoffman, H. et al. 1988. Risk for SIDS: Results of NICHD SIDS cooperative epidemiological study. *Ann NY Acad Sci* 533:13-30.

Jelliffe, D. and Jelliffe, E. F. P. 1978. *Human Milk in the Modern World.* Oxford: Oxford University Press.

Keens, T. G. and Van der Hol, A. L. 1984. Use of hypoxic and hypercarbic arousal responses in evaluation of infant apnea. *Perinatol Neonatol* 8:32.

Leistner, H. L. et al. 1980. Heart rate and heart rate variability during sleep in aborted sudden infant death syndrome. *J Pediatr* 97:51.

McCulloch, K. et al. 1982. Arousal responses in near-miss sudden infant death syndrome and in normal infants. *J Pediatr* 101:911.

McKenna, J. J. et al. 1993. Infant-parent co-sleeping in an evolutionary perspective: Implications for understanding infant sleep development and SIDS. *Sleep* 16:263-82.

McKenna, J. J. and Mosk, S. S. 1994. Sleep and arousal, synchrony and independence among mothers and infants sleeping apart and together (same bed): An experiment in evolutionary medicine. *Acta Paediatr Suppl* 397:94-102.

Mitchell, E. A. et al. 1991. Results of the first year of the New Zealand cot death study. *NZ Med J* 104:72-76.

Naeye, R. L. 1976. Sudden infant death temperament before death. *J Pediatr* 88:511.

Sears, W. 1995. *SIDS: A Parent's Guide to Understanding and Preventing Sudden Infant Death Syndrome.* Boston: Little, Brown.

Weissbluth, M. 1982. Sleep apnea, sleep duration and infant temperament. *J Pediatr* 101:307.

West, L. J. 1969. Foreword to *Dream Psychology and the New Biology of Dreaming,* ed. Melton Kramer. Springfield, Illinois: Charles C. Thomas.

# Chapter 13
## Nap Time: Your Link to Sanity

"My child doesn't seem to need a nap, but I sure do," revealed a tired mother of a busy two-year-old. Naps are usually necessary for babies and children to thrive and for mothers to survive.

## How Often Does a Baby Need to Nap?

The newborn has recently emerged from an environment that is visually subdued and filled with consistent rhythmic sounds. In his new environment the visual and auditory stimuli are unfamiliar, startling, and often overwhelming. When his senses become overloaded, which happens frequently, the newborn copes by falling asleep. He takes many short naps, measured in minutes, throughout the day. In addition to cat-napping, baby will have several longer periods of daytime sleep. By three months a baby's daytime sleep patterns are usually organized into two nap periods, one in the morning, one in the afternoon. Most babies will continue a pattern of a one-hour nap in the morning and a one- to two-hour nap in the afternoon throughout the remainder of the first year. Between one and two years, most babies drop the morning nap but still require a one- to two-hour afternoon nap. Most children require at least a one-hour afternoon nap up to age four.

Sleep researchers feel that napping does indeed have restorative value. Children and adults who nap may fall asleep more quickly and sleep more efficiently during the short period of time off during the day than they do at night.

### Nap When Your Baby Naps
In order for a mother to refuel her energies, she should learn to nap (and be encouraged to nap) when her baby does. It is a mistake to use baby's nap times to catch up on housework. You need the nap just as much as baby does. This is part of getting in harmony with your baby, in order that you both survive and thrive during those early exhausting months.

## Encouraging Naps

### Nap-Time Signs
A mother who is sensitive to her baby's cues will notice when he seems to need a nap. He may not actually need sleep, but his behavior is such that you know that he needs some time out. Previously happy and playful, he may gradually (or suddenly) begin to fuss or seem out of sorts, or he may start over-reacting to stimuli (too much noise or too much to see). He may need a little "down" time, quiet rocking with a lullaby and some soothing touching, or some nursing, maybe even lying down together. The baby may or may not fall asleep. Don't expect this down-time always to result in a nice stretch of sleep, or you will set yourself up to feel angry when those little eyes just don't close. The time may not be right now. You may need to give your baby another hour or so to play before he truly needs and can accept sleep. This little time-out can help him regain his happy nature so you'll both enjoy each other. You will see the definite signs of readiness for a nap later: more crankiness, droopy eyelids, slowing down, putting his head down, wanting to nurse.

### Conditioning Your Baby to Nap
Nap time can lend itself to conditioning if that's what fits your lifestyle. Some families operate better having a consistent time of the day for naps. Children can learn to sleep or at least to

*Nap nook.*

rest during these set times. Children cannot be forced to sleep, but you can set the stage for a sleep-inducing environment that allows sleep to overtake the child: a dark, quiet place, sleep-inducing music, lying down with your child. Breastfeeding toddlers seem to nap more eagerly because they anticipate this time of the day, so when these sleep-enticing conditions occur, sleep naturally follows. An example of this conditioning is the afternoon nap for the toddler which follows a usual sequence: lots of exercise, followed by lunch, followed by a story, followed by sleep-inducing music or a lullaby in a darkened, quiet environment. When the child gets used to these conditioning steps that lead up to a nap, sleep usually follows. Conditioning of the toddler and older child is easier if begun in early infancy.

Instead of having set and consistent nap times, some families have more flexible and unpredictable lifestyles, and their babies learn to nap on the run, in baby carriers and car seats. This is particularly true of large families. I remember when our one-and-a-half-year-old daughter, Erin, became accustomed to napping in her car seat during the afternoon car pool time.

**Nap times.** Early risers are usually ready for an early morning nap and an early afternoon nap. These are babies who are ready for bed early in the evening, at seven or eight o'clock. Another nap pattern may fit more realistically with today's busy lifestyles. If a baby can be enticed to sleep longer in the morning and take a late-morning and a late-afternoon nap, he would be more likely to be awake and happy during the prime evening time when father is home. Encouraging baby to nap early in the afternoon ("so he'll be tired and go to bed early and we finally have some time to ourselves") doesn't always work and deprives father of prime time with a well rested baby. In my own family we found that late afternoon naps worked the best. When I came home I was greeted by a well rested and playful baby.

"How can I schedule my baby's nap times?" tired and busy mothers often ask. If set nap times are your preference, you will be more successful if you schedule naps for yourself. Begin napping with your baby at set times each day. Eventually your baby may fall into a predictable nap-time pattern, even if you don't always nap with him.

### Enticing the Resistant Napper

Some babies are notoriously resistant to naps and do not allow themselves to fall asleep at a set time each day. There will be times when you know beyond a doubt that baby needs sleep, but he just won't give up. Many babies do not resist a nap, but they do resist napping alone. Since the natural state for babies is motion, not stillness, napping on the run may be the solution. Put your nap-resisting baby into a front or back carrier, sling, swing, bouncy buggy, or car seat and let the movement lull him to sleep.

Nap time does not always mean sleep time for the nap-resistant older toddler or child. It may suffice to establish a quiet time in the afternoon when the child lies down and listens to a record or story. This is marketed as "special time," a time when mommy (or daddy) and child simply rest and nest together.

### Nap Nooks

Be flexible about where your child is allowed to nap. Children are often reluctant to take naps; by not insisting that a child nap in his own bedroom you eliminate some hassles. Some children will crash for a nap anywhere in the house. The reluctant sleeper may be enticed by a "nap nook," a special place in a corner on a mat, a little tent made of blankets, a large box with one side cut out into which the child crawls when he is tired. This technique capitalizes on children's natural desire to construct their own little retreats in all the nooks and crannies throughout the yard and house.

Lambskin mats are also a good place for babies to nap and a way to condition them to sleep. I have seen mothers take the lambskin with them wherever they go. When baby is placed on the lambskin "bed," he takes a nap.

### When Sibling Naps Don't Match

The following is a common complaint from tired mothers: "I hear the advice 'nap when your baby naps,' but I can't because our six-month-old and our two-and-a-half-year-old do not nap at the same time. When my baby takes his nap I would love to join him, but it seems like this is just the time when our older child demands equal time from me. I feel strung out between both of our children's demands."

One of the most difficult parts of maturing as a parent is to realize that you can't always be all things to all of your children. Parenting is a bit of a juggling act where you try to give each child what he needs according to his stage of development, your energy permitting. Although mothers do seem to defy many laws of mathematics, you just can't give one hundred percent to each child all the time. You may need to call in some reserves. In this case, you might get your two-and-a-half-year-old involved in a play group for a few afternoons each week. When possible, mom and dad can do shift work. Dad takes the older child while mother naps when the baby naps.

If both your tiny baby and toddler are home at the same time, you may put the older child down for quiet time and turn on some records or get him started on some quiet play activity. If he is confined to a safe area with access to you should you be needed, you can lie down with baby. This arrangement usually allows the mother to doze with the tiny baby while at the same time keeping one ear open for her "resting" toddler.

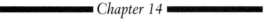 

# Chapter 14

# Preparing the Nest: Furniture for Sleep

Shortly after the birth of our fifth child our home was part of a tour benefiting a local charity. On one day of the tour my wife approached a puzzled looking grandmother and asked her, "Are you looking for something?" The guest replied, "Yes, I would like to see the baby's nursery." My wife held out her arms and proudly exclaimed, "It's right here."

It is not necessary to spend a lot of time and money preparing the properly appointed nursery. Your baby could care less what his or her room looks like. He wants you. Your arms, chest, voice, and bed are all the nursery baby really needs. But if you want nursery furniture, here are some suggestions.

## Cradles

Cradles are a wonderful invention for inducing sleep. As your baby squirms during a vulnerable period for awakening, the rocking of the cradle may lull him back to sleep. The baby-soothing business has tried to improve upon the swinging cradle by adding a wind-up mechanism to keep the cradle swinging and even "singing." Our modern swinging cradles are the counterpart of the hammocks used to soothe babies in other cultures. Some babies can be put down into the cradle half asleep and induced into a deeper sleep by gentle rocking.

Most babies need to fall asleep in the parents' bed or in their arms and then be transferred into a cradle when they are in the state of deep sleep. Rocking in general, whether in your arms or in a cradle, should be around sixty beats per minute, the heartbeat rhythm that your baby has grown accustomed to. Babies are usually ready to graduate from a cradle to a crib around six months of age when they begin sitting and peering over the edge.

# Cribs

Graduating from a cradle to crib may cause some temporary changes in sleep patterns as baby adjusts to the new bed. Keeping the sleep objects (blankets, lambskin, music box, heartbeat rhythm devices) baby was accustomed to in the cradle will help soothe the transition. The crib is motionless: if your baby needs the swaying movements of the crib, springs can be installed on the legs of the crib. Where to put the crib? Again, use the sleeping arrangement in which the whole family sleeps best. The crib can be put in your room, the baby's own room, a sibling's room, or consider the side-car arrangement described below.

## How to Buy a Safe Crib

1. *Look for a label from the Consumer Product Safety Commission or the Juvenile Products Manufacturer's Association (JPMA) stating that the crib conforms to safety standards.*

2. *Crib slats should be no more than 2⅜ inches (6 cm) apart to prevent the infant's body from slipping through the slats, leaving him hanging by his head and strangling. Cribs manufactured before 1979 may have more widely spaced bars.*

3. *The mattress should be firm and should fit the crib perfectly so that the infant's face cannot become wedged between the mattress and the sides of the crib, causing suffocation. To check the fit, push the mattress into one corner of the crib, then look at the gap between the mat-*

*tress and the crib at the opposite corner. There should be
no more than a 1½-inch (4 cm) space between the mattress and the side or end of the crib. If you can fit more
than two fingers between the mattress and the crib,
the mattress is too small. Another mattress should not be
substituted for the one designed by the manufacturer of
the crib.*

4. *Bumper pads keep baby's feet from dangling through the
slats and allow baby to push off with his feet and propel
himself around the crib. Crib bumpers should fit the crib
snugly around the entire perimeter and should be secured
by at least six ties or snaps. If the ties are long, trim them.
Remove the bumpers when your baby is able to pull up
holding on to the side of the crib. Bumpers can be used as
a step for climbing or tumblng over the rail.*

5. *Check baby's height when he is standing on the mattress
against the side rail. Once the height of the side rail is less
than three-quarters of the infant's height (baby's head and
neck are higher than the rail), the baby is too tall to be left
safely alone in the crib.*

6. *To prevent scratching the infant and catching his clothing,
metal hardware should be smooth and should not pro-
trude into the crib. Check the mattress support system frequently, pushing down from the top and up from the bottom to be sure that the metal hangers are securely locked
into the notches on the crib posts.*

7. *Latches on the drop side of the crib should be secure. Baby
should not be able to release them from the inside.*

8. *Toys that could serve as steps for the infant to climb out of
the crib should be removed as soon as the baby is able to
pull up on the crib rails.*

9. *The crib should not be placed against a window, near any
dangling ropes (i.e., cords from mini-blinds), nor near any
furniture which could be used to help the infant climb out
of his crib. The crib should be placed so that if your infant
climbs out of the crib, he would not fall against any sharp
object or become entrapped and possibly strangled
between the crib and the adjacent wall or furniture.*

10. *Any string longer than eight inches attached to a toy, mobile, pacifier, or clothing should not be in the crib or within reach of the infant. Strings can strangle.*

11. *Avoid cribs with ornate tops. Infants have strangled in the concave space between the post and the crib.*

12. *If the nursery is not within hearing distance of every room in the house (mothers have exceptionally good hearing), an intercom may prove a valuable safety feature.*

13. *Do not leave a baby unattended with a bottle propped up to feed himself.*

14. *Buttons on clothing can become entangled in the mesh of a mesh crib or playpen.*

15. *Cribs should be painted with a lead-free paint. Cribs manufactured after 1974 should conform to the regulations of the Hazardous Substance Act. Pamphlets about crib safety are available from the U. S. Consumer Product Safety Commission.*

## What to Look for in a Crib

1. *Adjustable springs permit adjustment of the mattress for your convenience and to accommodate baby's changing height. The height of the side rails above the mattress should be at least three-quarters of the height of the baby.*

2. *Drop rails on both sides give you more flexibility in positioning the crib. Be sure the side rails can be easily removed so that the crib can be used as a sidecar next to your bed. Good quality cribs are equipped with a steel stabilizing bar on both sides so that a railing can be removed and the stability of the crib still maintained.*

3. *Rail locks should be of the safety type requiring that the rail be slightly lifted before the lock releases and allows the rail to descend.*

4. *Plastic teething strips attached to the top of the side rails provide a chewing surface that is easy to keep clean and that prevents baby from sinking his teeth into the wooden rail.*

5. *Noiseless bearings help eliminate squeaks and disturbing noises when the side rails are raised and lowered. Your whole bedtime ritual can be defeated by raising a noisy crib rail just after you put your sleeping baby down.*

6. *Be sure the head and foot of your baby's crib have large free-rolling casters. This makes it easy to move the crib from place to place within baby's room or your room. It also enables parents to roll the crib back and forth slightly to gentle the baby to sleep.*

## What to Look for in a Good Crib Mattress

Mattresses are available in two basic constructions: coiled innerspring and foam rubber. Spring mattresses tend to be more expensive than foam. The price of coiled mattresses is usually determined by the number of coils and their individual construction. The two most important qualities to look for in the proper mattress for your baby are the quality of the cover and the firmness of the mattress. Good quality mattresses have triple-laminated cloth or plastic covers which are waterproof and easily cleaned of stains and odors. If the cloth, plastic, or vinyl covering is too thin it will wear easily, tear easily, and may not be waterproof. The mattress cover should also be flame-retardant.

The firmness of the mattress is best tested by using the entire palm of your hand, not just the fingertips. You should feel the proper balance between firmness and resiliency. A good quality mattress will have sufficient layers of felt and/or foam between the cover and the springs so that you cannot feel the springs. A foam mattress which is four to five inches thick will usually provide sufficient firmness to be comfortable and safe for the baby, although in theory, the weight distribution and support are better in a spring mattress. Whether this advantage is real depends upon the size and weight of your baby and the quality of the foam.

## Safe Bedding

Babies should sleep on firm surfaces. Avoid waterbeds, beanbags, squishy foam mats, or any other surface that could obstruct baby's breathing passages. Spread crib sheets smoothly, so there are no large wrinkles. Flannel-backed rubber pads are warm and prevent soiling of the underlying sheets and mattress cover. Use oversheets and blankets large enough to tuck under the sides and lower edge of the mattress, but don't tuck them so tightly that baby can't move. If your baby is prone to allergies, avoid bedding that collects lint, such as deep-pile lambskins or fuzzy wool blankets. Stuffed toys collect dust, which can irritate a baby with respiratory allergies.

Be especially vigilant about sleep safety when baby is sleeping somewhere other than his crib. Most parents give considerable thought to a safe sleeping environment at home in baby's own room. Observe the same precautions when baby is sleeping in a carriage or stroller, or when you are in a hotel room or visiting friends or family.

## The Most Important "Baby Furniture"

If you decide to buy a crib, do be sure it's a safe one. But keep in mind that neither cribs nor fancy cradles are absolutely essential. One mother reported that her baby stayed in the parental bed or a nearby cradle until around eight months. When she was introduced to her crib, she appeared to accept the crib quite happily, but by nine months of age this little climber had mastered the art of escape, even from the lowest mattress position. She was then provided with a mattress on the floor beside her older sister. A crib is a pretty big investment if it's destined for just one month's use! The most important "baby furniture" is a king-size bed and two open and accepting parents.

**Reference**

Sears, W. 1995. *SIDS: A Parent's Guide to Understanding and Preventing Sudden Infant Death Syndrome.* Boston: Little, Brown.

# Chapter 15

# Single Nighttime Parenting

It is very common for children to experience sleep disturbances following the death of a parent, divorce, or prolonged parental absences. When the harmony of a two-parent family (even one in which there is marital discord) is interrupted, the child's behavior is disrupted, especially his sleep cycles. Nap times become more unpredictable, bedtime rituals more prolonged, and night-waking becomes more frequent. Coping with these nighttime stresses is particularly difficult for the single parent who is also going through some readjustments. The goal of a single nighttime parent is to smooth the transition for the child.

## Consistency

As much as possible try to minimize the changes in your child's lifestyle: home, neighborhood, beds, and babysitters. Babies and children of all ages get used to routine in the family lifestyle. Too many changes too fast are guaranteed to produce a night-waker. Nap-time difficulties are usually encountered in addition to frequent night-waking. Besides the changes in the secure environment after a divorce or separation, the child is now very likely sleeping at two different homes and is expected to adapt his sleep rhythms to two different lifestyles. It is common for children not to sleep well in either home. The child may awaken frequently at the custodial parent's home out of fear that this parent may also leave. He awakens frequently at the non-custodial parent's home because he is required to sleep in a different bed and sometimes is not permitted to sleep with the parent, which he may be accustomed to doing at his more familiar home.

Expect signs of insecurity. Following the break-up of a marriage, it is very common for a child to cling to the custodial parent, mainly because of fear that this parent may also leave. It is usual for children not to want to nap alone, go to bed alone, or sleep alone. Even tiny babies sense a change in the family routine; this accounts for their sleep disturbances. Fears often keep the older child awake. "What will happen next? Is Mommy going to leave too?" Blaming themselves ("Did I cause Daddy to leave?") also keeps children awake.

Be open to your child's cues that he needs security. It is very normal and very healthy for a previously independent toddler to be glued to mommy now. If your baby or toddler wants to sleep with you, welcome your child into your bed at least for a few months, during the adjustment period. For the older child, a mattress alongside your bed will usually suffice. Remember though, that a child is not a substitute for an absent mate. The sleeping arrangement fulfills the needs of the child, not the adult. Older children are especially sensitive to the custodial parent leaning on them for security when they themselves are insecure. A certain amount of this mutual support is normal in single families, as long as a healthy balance is achieved.

When the child sleeps at the non-custodial parent's home, it helps to take a familiar attachment object along, such as a favorite blanket or a teddy bear. If the young child is accustomed to sleeping with the custodial parent, continue this sleeping arrangement with the other parent if possible. Both parents need to agree on consistent nap times, bedtimes, and sleeping arrangements.

Anticipate that the most difficult sleep problems will occur on the night that the child changes homes. The custodial parent will often report that "after a weekend with Daddy it took several nights to get him to sleep through again." One of the reasons for this sleep disturbance is the different lifestyle in the two homes. The custodial parent, usually the mother, is required to be the disciplinarian and usually runs a tighter ship with consistent nap times and bedtimes. The non-custodial parent, usually the father, may assume the role of "Disneyland Daddy" and create an undisciplined environment of junk food and unstructured sleep times. This confusion of lifestyles upsets the already confused child who requires several days to readjust. Some mutual agreement on maintaining the consistency of lifestyles will help lessen this confusion.

# Chapter 16

# Nighttime Parenting in Special Situations

There are many situations which directly affect children's sleep habits. Even though society is changing (a defense used to justify many diverse parenting styles), children's needs are not changing. Children are highly resilient, yet some children do not adapt to change as well as others. Recognizing the needs of children in special situations can help them adjust to change as well as make your nighttime parenting more effective.

## Working Mothers

If a mother returns to a full-time or part-time job outside the home, she should anticipate some changes in her child's sleep patterns. A good example is a mother who returns to work when her child is about a year old. She picks the child up at the babysitter around six o'clock, and the sitter boasts, "My, what a good baby. He slept all afternoon." At home the child is reluctant to go to bed. He awakens frequently during the night and does not resettle well. This change of sleep patterns is most exhausting for the mother who, because she has recently taken on extra work, usually needs extra sleep. In reality the child is tuning out the babysitter during the day and making up for the missed time with mom during the night. Babies have ways of extracting what they need from the modern system of child care. Working mothers may find that the child wants to sleep in the parents' bedroom or bed, and certainly any sleeping arrangement which gives the whole family more sleep should be respected. This is a situation in which you do what you feel you have to do during the day and you do the best you're able during the night. Studies have shown an increased incidence of sleeping difficulties in children of mothers who work outside the home (Campbell 1981). My advice to working mothers is to be more flexible and accepting of children's nighttime needs and sleeping arrangements just as they expect the children to be resilient and adaptable to the changes in care during the day.

## Mixed-Up Days and Nights

*"Our nine-month-old baby naps very well during the day, but at night she doesn't want to go to bed, awakens frequently, and doesn't resettle. I have recently returned to work. Could this be related?"*

Babies who take frequent naps during the day often wake a lot at night. Babies who take naps late in the afternoon often do not go to bed willingly at the "usual" bedtime of 8:00 P.M. Try to encourage a later afternoon nap and allow baby a more flexible bedtime; put him to bed when he needs to be put to bed, not when you want him to be put to bed. Around nine months of age, babies often go through a stage of separation anxiety. When your baby awakens at night, she does not want to be detached from you and put back down in bed alone. Your baby has not yet developed object permanence, the ability to realize that although you are out of sight, you are just around the corner in another room. To the nine-month-old, when you are out of sight you don't exist. Babies at this age do not separate from their mothers easily by day or by night. Yes, this may be related to your going back to work. Your baby may need to make up for the time spent away from you during the day by being awake at night.

## Substitute Nighttime Parenting

One of the inevitable questions parents ask is, "When can I leave my baby for a few nights?" Being able to leave your baby depends upon three variables:

1. *Your need to get away.*
2. *Your baby's sensitivity to separation.*
3. *The effectiveness of the substitute caregiver.*

In general I advise parents to travel as a threesome, at least for the first couple of years. If there are occasions in which you want to or must be away from your baby for a few days, please consider these suggestions for nighttime parenting:

*Try to make as few changes as possible in baby's day and nighttime routines.*

*Be sure you leave detailed instructions with the substitute caregiver about how you want your baby mothered during the day and during the night.*

*If your baby is used to sleeping with you, then continue having him sleep with somebody.*

*If your baby has certain nap-time routines, be sure to leave instructions for the substitute mother on how to mother the child to sleep.*

Because substitute caregivers often have different views of nighttime parenting than the baby's mother, it is absolutely necessary for you to hang tough on your principles of nighttime parenting: for example, describe in detail what the caregiver should do when your baby awakens during the night and cries.

## Traveling and Children

Parents will often report that during a family trip, baby did not sleep well and did not return to his original sleep patterns until several weeks after returning home. Some babies are quicker to adjust to change than others. High need babies are notoriously slow to adapt and prefer the security and consistency of one harmonious environment. Some parents report that their babies sleep better during a family vacation. I suspect that this may be due to the wider acceptance and greater relaxation that parents experience when they are away from the pressures competing for their attention at home. It is interesting that parents will occasionally report that their baby slept better on a trip because the motel did not have a crib and they had to let the baby sleep with them.

While traveling with baby, maintain consistency in nap times, parenting-to-bed rituals, and sleeping arrangements. If possible, take baby's bed along. A familiar blanket and sleep mate will usually provide a secure nighttime environment for a baby away from his usual bed. Home to a tiny baby is where his parents are, and this is especially true in nighttime parenting's family bed arrangement.

# The Baby Who Had a Rough Start

If your baby has been born prematurely, anticipate more frequent night-waking, at least for the first few months. Premature babies awaken more frequently because they are designed that way. Their night-waking is a survival and developmental mechanism. Premature babies have a higher percentage of REM or active sleep. Because the neurologic regulation of their breathing and cardiovascular systems is immature, premature babies need to be in a state in which they are more easily aroused for care and feeding. When your premature baby comes home from the hospital, anticipate frequent night-waking at least during the first few months.

### *Effect of Labor and Delivery on Baby's Sleep Patterns*

Studies have suggested that babies who are the product of a prolonged, difficult labor or who experience some distress during delivery showed a higher incidence of later sleep difficulties (Bernal 1973). It is possible that stress around the time of birth causes the newborn brain to lose its ability to maintain the state of quiet sleep (Schulte 1972).

# The Sick and Hospitalized Child

If possible, stay overnight with your child if he is in the hospital. Most hospitals now recognize the value of nighttime parenting and will offer parents the option of a cot next to their child's bed. Children definitely get well faster when they have unrestricted access to their parents.

There may be a night or two of broken rest when there is a sick baby or child in the house. A child who wakes up vomiting is really frightened; it certainly helps to be in close "waking" distance so you can be there to comfort your little one. A few sips of water or a little breastfeeding and a snuggle will help everyone settle back to sleep. A disturbing nighttime cough can be soothed with a dose of cough syrup recommended by your doctor. If you don't have any on hand, a teaspoon of honey in warm water (not for a child under one) can soothe a throat enough to let everyone get back to sleep. High fevers at night can cause a lot of concern. Everything seems worse in the dark. A dose of acetaminophen at bedtime and then again when the child awakes (at least three hours later) may keep the fever in check. Don't wake your child to give medication. If the temperature is over 103 degrees rectally and not affected by medication, a twenty-to-thirty minute soak in a lukewarm tub in the wee hours will help. If a child is upset, attend to him. Crying will only raise the fever.

An attack of croup (a seal-like, barking cough) in the nighttime is concerning the first time it happens. A steamy bathroom will ease the croupy breathing and break the panic reaction. Reading stories will help the croupy child relax.

Ear infections bother the child more at night because the prone position lets the fluid press on the sore inner ear. Analgesic ear drops and a dose of acetaminophen will help the pain. Let the child sleep upright, propped by several pillows. Again, being close to you helps ease the pain, so snuggle up.

**References**

Bernal, J. F. 1973. Nightwaking in infants during the first 14 months. *Develop Med Child Neurol* 15:760.

Campbell, K. 1981. Association of the domestic set-up with sleep difficulties in children under three years of age. *Med J Aust* 2:254.

Popper, B. 1998. *Babies and Children in the Hospital* (pamphlet). Schaumburg, IL: La Leche League International.

Schulte, F. et al, 1972. Maternal toxemia, fetal malnutrition. In *Sleep and the Maturing Nervous System,* ed. D. D. Clement. New York: Academic Press.

# Chapter 17

# A Closing Bedtime Story

There once was a baby who slept with his mother.

Before I was born, baby thought, I looked forward to nighttime. Mom was away from all those outside noises, and I could settle down and fall asleep to the sounds I had grown accustomed to and loved. Mommy sounds. Before birth we slept together, and it was good.

When I was born, my sleeping place changed, but my mother didn't. We still stayed together at night as we had for the past nine months. I was nervous about this new world that I didn't yet understand, but at night I wasn't afraid. Mommy and I slept together, and it felt good.

I like nighttime. During the day, Mommy has lots to do. But she's not so busy at night. She's always there, and I can snuggle up to her and nurse whenever I'm hungry. I have a tiny tummy and Mommy's milk is so easy to digest that I don't stay full very long. I need to eat very often. But because Mommy and I sleep together, I am never hungry very long and that feels good.

I don't know of any better place to sleep than with Mommy. I hear Aunt Nancy bought me a fancy crib. It has plastic animals that move when I touch them and metal bells that ring when I pull them. Some people think babies should sleep in cribs, but I don't think I'd like that. That crib doesn't move or talk or sing. It just creaks. And it's dark and hard and lonesome. Who would be there when I woke up? I like to reach over and touch Mommy during the night. I like how she feels and sounds. Aunt Nancy's real nice. We don't tell her that I don't like cribs. Mommy says I can throw my toys in it when I'm bigger. It will make a good cage for my stuffed bears and elephants. I'll go on sleeping with Mommy. It feels good.

I'm getting pretty big now. It takes a lot of energy to grow, so I'm eating more. It's a good thing that Mom's handy all night long because I really need all that good milk. Mommy's milk tastes better at night, maybe because she's so relaxed. I wake up often just to check that everything is okay. Then I have a little suck, but I don't bother anybody. I can grow real fast because I don't have to waste any energy worrying. I'm too little to worry anyway. Besides, I don't have to worry because Mommy and I sleep together and I feel good.

Sometimes Mommy has a bad day, and she has trouble falling asleep. But soon I start to nurse and you know what? She starts getting sleepy and sometimes she's sound asleep before I am. We help each other go to sleep. Because I sleep with Mommy, she feels good.

I have bad days sometimes, too, and bad nights. I get anxious and confused. My new teeth are hurting, my bottom burns, my nose gets stuffy. (Babies need clear noses to breathe, you know.) When I don't feel good it's comforting to reach over and touch Mommy or Daddy. I nurse a little and go back to sleep. We all feel better.

My mom's friends are always giving her books to read and telling her how she shouldn't run to me whenever I cry. They use awful sounding words like manipulation. Mommy just laughs and says that she reads me, instead of a book. I'm sure glad she listens to me. She's getting to be a better mother all the time. We sleep together, we trust each other, and we feel good.

I like going to bed. I get so much attention. There's nobody else around, just Mommy, Daddy, and me. Our bed isn't fancy, but there's room enough for all of us. Mommy tells Grandma not to spend a lot of money on fancy things for me. She brought over a teddy bear that made sounds like somebody's mother. It didn't sound like my mother, and when you held it, it didn't do anything. Why should a baby have to get used to the

sounds of someone else's mother? My favorite teddy bear is my mommy. She cuddles back when I hold on to her. At night we sleep together and touch each other and feel good.

I'm getting to know Dad better these days. I'm not sure he liked sleeping with me in the beginning. He's so big and I'm so tiny. We were both a little afraid. Besides, I was pretty noisy a few months ago. One night Dad even told Mom that it was time to make me sleep in that awful crib. I sure like sleeping with Daddy, and now he likes sleeping with me, too. I don't see him much during the day. He's very busy working. It's nice to be with him at night. Daddy and I sleep together, and we feel good.

I never have to cry very loud or long to get attention when I need something, even if all I want is to be held and talked to. I spend most of the day in Mommy's arms or in the baby sling next to Mommy. She knows that being with the people who love me makes me happy. If ever Mommy didn't pick me up when I cried, I don't know what I'd do. Get really mad, I guess. But I know the world is a nicer place than that. How could I ever feel good if Mommy left me alone in the dark? Everything feels right when we sleep together.

Someday I'll grow up and leave home, get married and have babies of my own. And do you know where they'll sleep? With me, of course. Is there any other way? We'll sleep together, and we'll feel good.

# About La Leche League

La Leche League International was founded in 1956 by seven women who wanted to help other mothers learn about breastfeeding. Today La Leche League is an internationally recognized authority on breastfeeding, with a mother-to-mother network that includes La Leche League Leaders and Groups in countries all over the world.

Mothers who contact LLL find answers to their questions on breastfeeding. They also find support from other parents who are committed to being sensitive and responsive to the needs of babies and small children. Local LLL Groups meet monthly to discuss breastfeeding and related issues. La Leche League Leaders are available by telephone and offer information and encouragement for women with questions about breastfeeding.

## Publications

La Leche League International distributes more than three million publications each year, including many other books by William and Martha Sears. If you have enjoyed NIGHTTIME PARENTING, you will also want to read THE FUSSY BABY: HOW TO BRING OUT THE BEST IN YOUR HIGH NEED CHILD, BECOMING A FATHER, *The Baby Book*, and *The Discipline Book*. These and other books by Dr. Sears offer additional information about the philosophy of attachment parenting applied to a multitude of situations.

For more information on breastfeeding, read La Leche League's how-to book, THE WOMANLY ART OF BREASTFEEDING, now in its sixth edition. You'll find more information on nursing past one year of age in MOTHERING YOUR NURSING TODDLER by Norma Jane Bumgarner and HOW WEANING HAPPENS by Diane Bengson.

Look for all of these titles in bookstores, or order them from La Leche League International.

- **Order publications by phone using your VISA or MasterCard.** Call 847-519-9585, or 847-519-7730 weekdays between 9 A.M. and 5 P.M. Central Time. Or fax your order to 847-519-0035.
- **You can write to LLLI at P. O. Box 4079, Schaumburg, IL 60168-4079.**
- **To find a Leader and a Group near you, check your local telephone book, or call 800-LA-LECHE in the USA.**
- **In Canada call 800-665-4324, or write to LLLC, 18C Industrial Drive, Box 29, Chesterville, Ontario.**
- Visit our web site at www.lalecheleague.org/